D1113851

TOUCHED BY THE FIRE

TOUCHED BY THE FIRE

edited by
Wayne E. Warner

Eyewitness Accounts of the
Early Twentieth-Century
Pentecostal Revival

Logos International
Plainfield, New Jersey

TO BERNEDA

TABLE OF CONTENTS

FOREWORD

For a long time I had hoped someone would put together a book of this nature. As I read it, I shouted and wept for joy as my heart hungered to see God move as He moved in that great day of yesteryear. Thank the Lord He is the same today and forever and that the great miracles we read about are still happening.

As I read many of these names and the experiences that took place in their lives and ministries so long ago, I knew these were people that God had specially honored with His power and His great touch. Some few of these people I had the honor and privilege of meeting.

A.A. Wilson was one. He was probably one of the greatest preachers of the gospel that ever lived. I had the honor of preaching with him in some of the last camp meetings he preached. Even though I was young enough to be his grandson, he took so much time with me and I like to feel that part of my ministry was inspired by this giant of the Faith. I called him the Apostle of Love.

Then there was Raymond T. Richey. When I was a little boy, I heard of this great Apostle of Faith and the great miracles that were being performed. Miracles that would boggle the mind. I never dreamed I would have the opportunity to meet him. God worked this out shortly before he went on to glory. I will never forget the last words he spoke to me. He was a man small in stature. As I stood there that day, he took both my hands in his. He seemed to look long and deep into my eyes. He started to talk about the Spirit of God. He seemed to come alive as the words flowed from his aged body. He said: "Young man, never forget the Holy Spirit is the one that does the work." A short time later Raymond T. Richey was called home to glory. He was one of the greatest men that ever lived. I never forgot his words.

E.L. Tanner was like a spiritual father to the state of Louisiana, my home state. I met him when I was just a kid.

His life was impeccable. He was the Father of Pentecost in our part of the world. I saw him just the other day. He is not too many years short of the century mark. He was bedridden but still full of faith and the Holy Ghost. His mind was sharp and clear. As we talked about the moving of the Holy Spirit his eyes fairly sparkled. That was all he knew to talk about and it was enough.

These are people that changed the destiny of a world. They allowed God to move through their hearts and lives. No man needs glory in the flesh, but thank God they allowed the Holy Spirit to move through them with mighty signs and wonders. I am a product of their ministries—millions are. Their names will never die and their messages will never wane. They shall ever shine as the brightness of the sun.

Jimmy Swaggart

TOUCHED BY THE FIRE

THE HEALING OF A TWENTIETH-CENTURY LAZARUS

Smith Wigglesworth

One day in the early 1900s I went to the top of a high mountain in Wales for a time of prayer. The Lord's presence seemed to envelop and saturate me, reminding me of the Transfiguration scene. I was impressed with the thought that the Lord's only purpose in giving us such glorious experiences is to prepare us for greater usefulness in the valley.

Little did I realize what the Lord had in store for me within the next few days.

Two years before there had come to our house in Bradford, England, two young men from Wales. They were just ordinary men, but they became very zealous for God. When they came to our mission in Bradford and saw some of the works of God, they said to me, "We would not be surprised if the Lord brings you to Wales to raise our Lazarus."

Lazarus, they explained, was the leader of their assembly. He had spent his days working in a tin mine and his nights preaching, and the result was that he had collapsed, gone into consumption, and for four years had been a helpless invalid, having to be fed with a spoon.

There on the mountaintop, two years after I had first heard of the man, the Lord said to me, "I want you to go and raise Lazarus." After going back to the valley I wrote a postcard to a man in the place whose name had been given to me by the two young men. I wrote: "When I was on the mountain praying today, God told me that I was to go and raise Lazarus."

Later when we arrived at the place we went to see the man to whom I had written the card. He looked at me and said, "Did you send this?" When I answered that I had sent the card, he said, "Do you think we believe in this? Here, take it." And he threw the card at me.

The man then called a servant and said, "Take this man to Lazarus." Then he turned to me and said, "The moment you see him you will be ready to go home. Nothing will hold you."

Everything he said was true from a natural view. The man was helpless. He was nothing but a mass of bones with skin stretched over them. There was no life to be seen. Everything in him spoke of decay.

I encouraged the man to believe. "You remember that at Jericho," I said, "the people shouted while the walls were still up. God has victory for you if you will only believe. Will you shout?"

But I could not get him to believe. There was not an atom of faith there. He had made up his mind not to have anything.

It is a blessed thing to learn that God's word can never fail. Never hearken to human plans. God can work mightily when you persist in believing Him in spite of discouragements from the human standpoint.

When I got back to the man to whom I had sent the postcard, he asked, "Are you ready to go now?" But I am not moved by what I see. I am *moved only by what I believe.*

There were difficult conditions in that Welsh village, and it seemed impossible to get the people to believe. . . . A couple asked us to stay with them. I asked the people in the village if any could pray. But no one wanted to pray. I asked for seven people to pray with me for the poor man's deliverance in a prayer meeting the next morning. I told the people that I trusted that some of them would awaken to their privilege and join us in prayer for the raising of Lazarus.

When I got to bed it seemed as if the devil tried to place on me everything that he had placed on that poor man. When I awoke I had a cough and all the weakness of a tubercular patient. I rolled out of bed . . . and cried out to God to deliver me from the power of the devil. I shouted loud enough to wake everybody in the house, but nobody was disturbed. God gave victory, and I got back in bed as free as ever. At five o'clock the Lord awakened me and said, "Don't break bread until you break it round My table." At six o'clock He gave me these words, "And I will raise him up."

I put my elbow into the fellow who was sleeping with me and said, "Do you hear? The Lord says that He will raise him up."

When we went to the house where Lazarus lived, there were eight of us. No one can prove to me that God does not always answer prayer. He always does more than that. He always gives the exceedingly abundant above all we ask or think.

I shall never forget how the power of God fell on us as we went into that sick man's room. Oh, it was lovely! As we circled the bed I got one brother to hold one of the sick man's hands and I held the other. Then we took the hand of the one next to us.

"We are just going to use the name of Jesus," I told them. We knelt down and whispered that one word, "Jesus! Jesus!

Jesus!" The power of God fell and then it lifted. Five times the power of God fell and then it remained. But the man in the bed was unmoved. Two years previous someone had come along and had tried to raise him up, and the devil had used his lack of success as a means of discouraging Lazarus. I said, "I don't care what the devil says; if God says He will raise you up, it must be so. Forget everything else except what God says about Jesus."

The sixth time the power fell and the sick man's lips began moving and the tears began to fall. I said, "The power of God is here; it is yours to accept."

Then he made a confession: "I have been bitter in my heart, and I know I have grieved the Spirit of God. Here I am helpless. I cannot lift my hands, nor even lift a spoon to my mouth."

"Just repent, and God will hear you," I told him.

He repented and cried out, "O God, let this be to Thy glory." As he said this the virtue of the Lord went right through him.

I have asked the Lord to never let me tell this story except as it was, for I realize that God cannot bless exaggerations.

As we again said, "Jesus! Jesus! Jesus!" the bed shook, and the man shook. I told the people who were with me that they could go downstairs. "This is all God. I'm not going to help him." I sat and watched that man get up and dress himself, and then we sang the doxology as he walked down the steps. I said to him, "Now tell what has happened."

It was soon noised abroad that Lazarus had been raised up and the people came from Llanelly and all the district round to see him and hear his testimony. And God brought salvation to many as he told the story in an open-air meeting. . . . All this came through the name of Jesus, through faith in His name. Yes, the faith that is by Him gave the sick man perfect health in the presence of the crowd.

PRESERVED THOUGH POISONED

F.D. Davis

Immediately after I was filled with the Spirit in May 1917, my wife and I went out into the country where there were no churches and began a revival. In a few weeks' time the Lord filled some forty people with the Spirit. Later that summer more than one hundred souls were filled with the Spirit in a community near Rusk, Texas, where we were preaching.

We also saw many healings from the Lord. Mrs. Annie Gardner had been bedfast for months. Her husband brought her to the meeting one evening in a wagon, on springs and mattress. When the altar call was given, she wanted to seek the Lord, so her husband brought her to the altar. There she was saved, healed, and filled with the Spirit. As she lay under the power of God, her physician, who was also in the congregation that night, came up to see about her. He took her pulse, then stepped back and said, "She is all right as long as she is under that Power." She was well from that time on.

We had many other experiences which encouraged our faith, but there were trials and opposition too. Once both our baby and I had malaria, but God would always make it possible for me to preach in the evening service even when I had chills during the day.

It was raining one morning when I arose from the bed—a thin quilt on the schoolroom floor. We were out of food, but even if we had a pantry full of food, we could not cook when it rained, because we had to cook outside. After we had prayed for food that morning, I walked to the door and looked out. I saw a man about half a mile away leaving his home with an umbrella over his head and a box under his arm. "Thank the Lord," I said, "He is sending us our breakfast."

A few minutes later the man came into the building and gave us the box. There before us was a prepared breakfast fit for a king—big hot biscuits, fried eggs, good country ham, and plenty of it. We expressed our gratitude for his kindness.

Several years later we met the daughter of the man who had brought the food. She told us that her father had given his heart to the Lord and was filled with the Spirit. He testified he could never get away from the thankfulness he saw on our faces that morning.

One evening during a brush arbor meeting at Huntsville, Texas, in 1924, the Lord led me to preach on Mark 16:17-18, which includes the promise, "If they drink any deadly thing, it shall not hurt them."

Unknown to us an unbeliever in the audience decided to test this at our expense. He took several other men with him and purchased a bottle of poison from a drugstore in the town. During the altar service they went to the house where we were staying and stirred the poison into the bucket of drinking water on the porch. The leader of the group hid out in the darkness to see what would happen.

When we arrived home, tired and thirsty after a lengthy altar service, we drank heartily of the water and went to bed. The man reported to his friends, "They will be dead in the morning." The next morning he hid out in the bushes near our house and was surprised to see that we were up and about as usual.

An extremely large crowd attended the service the next night, for those who had heard of the incident were curious.

Sometime later our son was pastoring a church in the same town when a man who had been saved came and said, "I have a confession to make." He then told of his being an accomplice in poisoning the water that night. This was our first knowledge of the incident.

One night while preaching in another city some distance away I made reference to the poisoned water. After the service a man I did not know came and said, "Brother Davis, I am the man who put the poison in the water and I saw you drink it. I want you to know that God has saved me and filled me with the Holy Spirit, and I am living for the Master today."

The God we serve has kept His word to us these many years, and I know He will keep it to the end.

3

GOD'S MOVING AT AZUSA MISSION

Rachel A. Sizelove

While my husband and I were attending a Free Methodist camp meeting in June, 1906, we heard there was a company of people in an old building, speaking in tongues as on the day of Pentecost. My husband passed by the building and heard such wonderful singing in the Spirit.

I went with him, and as we entered the old building, somehow I was touched by the presence of God. It was such a humble place with its low ceilings and rough floor. Cobwebs were hanging in the windows and joists. As I looked around I thought of Jesus when He came to earth and was born in a manger. There was no place for Him in the inn. I thought of the fine churches in Los Angeles, but the Lord had chosen His humble spot to gather all nationalities, to baptize them with the Holy Ghost.

The building was soon cleaned out and the ceilings were whitewashed. A large box served as the pulpit. William J. Seymour (one of the leaders) stayed behind the box on his knees before the Lord, hidden away from the eyes of the world so much of the time. Oh, how God used that old black brother and gave him wisdom as He did Moses to lead and teach the people.

The first afternoon I went there about twelve of God's children, white and black, were tarrying before the Lord, some sitting and some kneeling. My attention was especially drawn to two young men, a Brother Clifford and a Brother Johnson. (The latter soon after went to Sweden and later to Palestine as a missionary.) These two young men were sitting with eyes closed, with faces uplifted toward heaven. With a heavenly glow on their faces, they spoke in tongues to themselves and to God.

My soul cried out, "O Lord, these people have something I do not have."

Brother Seymour gave out the Word and made an altar call, inviting the people to seek the Lord for pardon or sanctification or the baptism in the Holy Spirit. I thought, "Well, praise God, he is not doing away with any of my experiences or beliefs but just adding to my experience—the baptism in the Holy Spirit, which he said could only come to a clean heart."

I went home and began to search the Word of God. I saw that it was in the Bible. And then I went again to the mission in July 1906. By that time crowds were beginning to gather. This time when Brother Seymour gave the altar call, I went with many others to the altar. Raising my hands toward heaven, I said, "Lord, I want my inheritance, the baptism in the Holy Spirit and fire." Instantly in the Spirit I saw as it were a bright star away in the distance and my very soul cried out to God. Oh, I knew it was God, and as He came nearer, He was in the form of a beautiful white dove. As He came so close I thought I was going to receive the baptism. I was then slain upon the floor. Then the Lord began to deal with me. I had died out to everything of which I knew and believed. I had a clean heart in the sight of God, but He asked me about my denomination. I said, "Lord, my church will receive anything that is from you." Then I was shaken by the power of God. . . . The Lord knew that my church would not receive the experience. So he had me die out to opinions of my church before He could baptize me with the Holy Spirit.

Later the Lord showed me that I must go to Springfield, Missouri, and tell my family what He had done for me. He wanted them to hear the blessed message. So in May 1907 my husband agreed that I should go to Springfield. Before leaving I went to the Azusa Street Mission and asked the believers to pray with me that the Lord would make His will plain. The evidence came so clearly: "My child, you may go and I will be with you." After the believers gathered around me and laid their hands on my head and prayed, they gave me a minister's license.

On the way to Springfield by train, I traveled with a dear black woman who had been at the Azusa Street Mission and who was on her way to carry the glad message to Africa. We talked with everyone we could about the mighty outpouring of the Holy Spirit. The conductor gave us permission to hold services on the train, and the people listened intently and many were convicted.

After arriving in Springfield, the Holy Spirit spoke through me in tongues and then gave the interpretation: "The Holy Spirit as a dove shall hover over this place."

Soon the neighbors came in to inquire about the great Pentecostal revival in Los Angeles. After telling them how the Lord baptized me with the Holy Spirit, I said, "We have been talking of the wonderful works of God. Let us kneel down and pray before you leave." And while I was praying, the Holy Spirit prayed through me in other tongues. When my sister heard me praying in tongues, she reached her hands toward heaven and cried, "O Lord, this is You, and I want the baptism in the Holy Spirit." She was slain under the mighty power of God and received the baptism, spoke and sang in tongues. She was the first to receive the baptism in Springfield. How precious and holy the very atmosphere seemed in that all-night meeting, June 1, 1907.

The power began to fall that night and has been falling ever since and will continue until Jesus comes. Hallelujah.

Editor's Note: In 1913 Rachel Sizelove returned to Springfield. One afternoon while alone in her sister's house, the Lord showed her a vision. "There appeared before me a beautiful, bubbling, sparkling fountain in the heart of Springfield," she later described it. "It sprang up gradually but irresistibly and began to flow toward the East and toward the West, toward the North and toward the South, until the whole land was deluged with living water." Mrs. Sizelove and others later understood this vision to be of the Assemblies of God and its publishing ministry which was organized in 1914 and moved to Springfield in 1918.

4

MY FIRST EARNEST PRAYER

J.K. Gressett

It was late spring in 1916 in a rough community twelve miles from town in central Texas when the rumor got around that some peculiar people were coming to hold a brush arbor meeting. Many tales accompanied the report as to what they preached and how they carried on. The peculiar people turned out to be the Rev. and Mrs. Frank R. Anderson, who did a great work for God in the South for many years.

My mother, who was an invalid, had used crutches for some years, and the doctor gave her no hope of being well again. She raised her family right and tried to live right. My father was a rugged, honest Texas farmer with no time for religion of any kind. But during this meeting I saw my father help my mother on her crutches down the straw-covered aisle to the altar.

Mother had followed the messages of the minister for several days as he preached full salvation, the baptism in the Holy Spirit with the evidence of speaking in tongues, divine healing, and the coming of the Lord. After a few minutes at the altar, one of her crutches went one way and the other another way. Mother came up the same aisle running and shouting, and father came right after her. This great miracle opened the way for a glorious revival that swept the country, for the entire community knew how sick my mother had been for so long. She was healed instantly, and received the baptism in the Holy Spirit a few nights later.

Brother Anderson had a water baptismal service at a ranch pond each Sunday for six weeks. One Sunday the wife and daughter of a tough ex-sheriff were to be baptized. That man paraded at the edge of the water before the crowd waving a large knife, saying, "If that preacher baptizes my wife I will cut his throat before he gets on dry ground." It really was a tense time, for people knew how mean he was. But his wife was baptized. When she came up out of the water shouting and speaking in tongues, the sheriff's knife went sailing over the pond dam and he hit the water, Stetson hat, boots, and all, crying, "Preacher, baptize me! My family is going to heaven and leave me!"

Brother Anderson fearlessly pushed him back saying, "I don't baptize people who have not repented." But the ex-sheriff replied, "I was saved since I left the bank." He was then baptized, along with a number of others who were saved while looking on.

When the Andersons started a meeting in another community twenty miles from our home, many of the believers went back and forth to help. The first person to receive the baptism there was John Hall who owned the little telephone exchange in the ranch community. For days he never answered "Hello." Instead, there was a clear loud "Hallelujah" on the line every time someone called. It helped stir that community to the extent that about 100 were saved and baptized in the Spirit.

After these great meetings the evangelists went to other places to minister. The people held cottage prayer meetings, some of which lasted nearly all night. My father bought seven Bibles at one time for use around the family altar. But with parents and brothers and sisters saved, I stubbornly held out to enjoy worldly pleasures, or so I thought.

After attending a dance on a Saturday night I would often find Mother praying in the corn shucks in the barn when I put my saddle away. On cold nights she would be by the kitchen stove, always praying for her wayward boy. I would say, "Mother, get some rest. The Lord will save me when He gets ready." Her answer was, "Son, I think He is about ready." A powerful sermon it was.

In 1918 when influenza was taking entire families, I was the only one to get it in our family. We had gone to another county to work because of dry weather. After three weeks with flu and double pneumonia, I was given less than eight hours to live. I gave in and asked for someone to come and pray for me. They could not find a minister who believed in divine healing, so my father phoned home and two farmers and the telephone exchange man came, driving through a snowstorm all day in an open Model T Ford. It was dark when they arrived, and they were very cold. It broke my heart to see men do so much good for a "no-good" like me.

My first real earnest prayer was, "Lord, if there is any more love like that I sure need it." I believe He heard my prayer. As those brethren with my family prayed around that bed in the little log cabin, there was a red glow in the ceiling as if a hole had been burned in the roof. A bright light appeared and I reached for it. As I did, it enveloped me like a warm shower from my head down. Every pain left; every sin was gone. I spoke in other tongues for an hour and a half. I felt so light and clean inside and out. I was up for breakfast the next morning, though I had had no food for four days, had lost 30 pounds, and suffered constantly.

I would not exchange conversions with Saul of Tarsus. I was there when God saved me and it's as real today as it was in 1918.

5

I HEARD THE ANGELS SING

Arthur F. Berg

I was not dreaming. I did not have a vision. I was wide awake that day, when suddenly the room was filled with the sound of singing—voices and music blending in beautiful harmony. Where was it coming from? How? Why?

We were alone on a pioneer mission station at Masisi-Rutchuru in the Kivu District of the Congo. For many days, my wife and our little daughter Agnes had been ill with the deadly malaria fever. After holding for several days at 104 degrees, Mrs. Berg's temperature rose to 105.2. In her weakness, her voice was but a faint whisper, and at times she seemed to be drifting into a semi-coma. I knew her condition was critical, so I called in a group of Congolese Christians to pray with me. They readily responded and prayed earnestly. I was touched by their faith and loyalty, yet the feeling of depression did not leave. *Oh, if I only had a fellow missionary!*

After a while I stepped out of our humble thatched-roof home into the African night. It was one of those clear tropical moonlit nights with myriads of stars seemingly suspended from the heavens. They looked so near, as if one could just reach up and touch them.

I looked toward the northwest—our home in the United States, ten thousand miles away. "O God," I prayed. "Does anyone at home know our predicament? Does anyone care?"

Years later, after returning to America, I got the answer. A little lady in Minneapolis, a friend of our family, asked me, "Were you and Anna in special need at this certain time in the Congo?"

Then she continued, "I saw your face before me. I was seized with a tremendous burden. I went to God in prayer and prayed till peace and assurance of His answer filled my heart."

We compared dates and learned it was the exact time when I was out in the night, praying and crying to God from a breaking heart.

But on that dark night I knew nothing of this. I went back into the house where the African Christians were still faithfully praying. I urged them to continue while I sat down by our little folding pump organ and began to play. Opening a hymnbook I saw the song, "Was There Ever a Friend So True?" It was not a familiar song, but as I sang it the words seemed directed to me. One verse says:

He soothes me in sorrow with songs in the night,
And inspires me with hope anew;
He fills me with courage my battles to fight,
Was there ever a friend so true?

I needed the Lord's assurance in that hour. I sang on and on, pouring out my soul to God in the words of the song.

Suddenly the room seemed filled with indescribable music. I was no longer alone! I was aware of a divine presence. A choir, the beauty of which I never heard before or since, was singing. They were singing of Christ, a Friend who was near. For a moment I was startled. I looked around. The Congolese Christians were still in prayer, and anyway I remembered that they could not sing in English. I turned back to the organ and joined with the invisible choir in singing glory and praise to God. My heart was lifted up and I knew the Lord was very near.

This rapturous moment was interrupted as a door was flung open and someone called excitedly, *"Madamu, anakufa, Madamu, anakufa!"* (Madam is dying! Madam is dying!) A houseboy who had been watching in the sickroom was standing before me, fear and grief mingled in his face.

Urging the Christians to continue in prayer, I went quickly to my wife. Instead of finding her dying, I saw and heard her praising God, speaking in tongues with a clear and steady voice. Her hands were lifted up in worship and adoration to our wonderful Lord. I knelt and joined with her in thanks to God. I then felt her forehead and found it wet with perspiration. The fever had broken. As we continued to praise God together, her temperature continued to come down.

Later Anna said that in the midst of her suffering it had seemed that a ball of fire touched her head and went through her entire body. Its warmth was greater, but so different from the burning fever. The Lord's presence filled her heart, and praises to God naturally followed. God had touched and healed her, and from that moment she regained strength. At the same time our little daughter was also healed. (*Editor's note:* Agnes grew up and married D.V. Hurst, now president of Northwest College, Kirkland, Washington.)

It had all taken place simultaneously. When I was out in the yard praying, when the African Christians were interceding, and when the little lady in Minnesota also prayed, the answer came. A choir of angels was sent to strengthen a weary missionary with their heavenly singing! My wife and daughter were restored to health. Truly we serve a blessed Lord, a true and wonderful *Friend*.

6

GOD HEALED MY FATHER

A.M. Alber

It was in the spring of 1914, a very pleasant time of the year as far as weather was concerned. But it was not a happy time in our central Kansas home. My father, Jacob Alber, had been a very hard-working man. Now at sixty he was close to death with heart trouble and hardening of the arteries.

For months his condition had been critical, and now the doctors said he would not live another week. There were twelve of us children. Father called us all in and gave instructions as to how to carry on after his departure.

I was very disturbed about my father's illness and would often go into the field to pray earnestly that God would heal him. I was a sinner, but I prayed. Over and over again I would plead, "O God, heal my father, and I will serve you." I was in real agony at times, and the tears flowed freely.

Our family attended church regularly, so when a minister came from the hills of Tennessee to hold a revival in one of the two churches in our community, he soon learned of Father's illness. The minister, believing in divine healing, came with some men of the community to visit my father and pray for him. Faith began to rise in Father's heart. The minister returned in a couple of days with men from both of the churches. These men gathered around Father's bed and prayed for his healing.

Watching from the dining room I was surprised to see my father get out of bed and kneel with the others. After prayer he walked into the room where I was and sat down. He had taken no solid food for some time, yet he ate supper that evening. The next morning he was up early and called us boys to breakfast!

As the meetings continued, people came from far and near to see the man who had been so wonderfully healed. Attendance at the revival increased until they had to move into a large conference tent. Many were saved. Many were prostrated under the power of God. Some had visions. Two weeks after my father's healing I was saved, and many of my friends were also saved in that meeting.

The following year two men came from California bringing the message of the baptism of the Holy Spirit with the evidence of speaking in other tongues. I was among the number who opened their hearts to this message, and was filled with the Holy Spirit. The men moved on to other places, and that fall I was called upon to preach to the newly filled church.

What a joy it has been these more than fifty years to preach the gospel with the Holy Ghost sent down from heaven.

A VISION FOR THE LOST

Marie E. Brown

I remember October 18, 1906, when the Lord baptized me in the Holy Spirit. For six hours He moved upon me in intercessory prayer for various mission fields.

First He took me to China. I saw high stone walls and from beyond them heard the Chinese crying for help. As I prayed, it seemed stone after stone came out of the walls, and I saw a great multitude of Chinese waiting to hear the message of salvation. Then the Lord took me to India. There I saw the people of different castes, and I wondered and wept. But even as I wept for India's lost, the Lord showed me the continent of Africa. I preached to those people and they were especially responsive. Then in a vision I went to Japan. There I entered an orphanage, and one by one the children came to me.

Each of these fields was laid heavily upon my heart, and it seemed God was calling me to service in one of them. While I was waiting upon the Lord to know to which field He would have me go, I was asked to come to New York. And this became my mission field all these years.

Since I had the vision of foreign missions in my heart,

Glad Tidings Tabernacle (New York City) soon became a missionary church. Its great burden through the years has been to send the gospel into all the world. Missionaries have been sent to each field represented in my vision, and to others besides. That which has been sown continues to bear fruit both at home and beyond the seas, and occasions this time of mutual rejoicing.

Editor's note: Carl Brumback, writing in his book *Suddenly . . . From Heaven,* gives us more information on the author, her husband Robert, and the church they pastored. "What a team God joined together! For many years they labored together in the heart of the great American metropolis. Glad Tidings Tabernacle, located on West 33rd Street, just across from the Pennsylvania Station, has been the means of multitudes of souls finding Christ. Scores of ministers have gone forth into the harvest field. One of the most remarkable features of this church is its missionary spirit. Year after year the sacrificial giving of the people has furthered the full gospel in the regions beyond. Surely, God knows what He is doing! When He commands one who would go to the foreign field to stay, He does not take away the missionary vision, but multiplies it."

8

LIVING BY FAITH
IN EGYPT

Lilian Trasher

God put it on the heart of one of His children to send me an offering (for the Assiut Orphanage). So, faithful to the "still small voice," this dear brother away over in Kansas went down to his bank and made out a check . . . and wrote a letter. But as often happens, this dear brother in addressing the letter to me made a great mistake. He addressed it to "Assiut, India" instead of "Assiut, Egypt."

So when the thousands of letters were being placed in the mail bags ready to be put on the ships to India or Egypt, our loving Father knew that this letter must not go to India as directed but must be sent to Egypt, or our babies would have to go without bread. So He took care of it and had it put into one of the Egypt mail bags even though Egypt was nowhere written on the letter! It was not delayed a single day.

On the afternoon of the day of our great need one of our little boys went to the post office and found the letter which God had taken care of. He brought it home and I opened it. It contained the check for $1,000! I cannot describe the joy of us all as we saw how God had supplied our needs. We paid $600 which we owed, paid the $300 in salaries, and had $100 to go on. How everyone in town who heard this rejoiced with us! "Before they call, I will answer."

There was another time we were in great need, and I could think of nothing that I could do; so I went to my English teacher and asked her if she would lend me $25 for a few days. She said, "Why, certainly. Do come in and sit down and let me make you a cup of tea."

While she was making the tea (she had not yet given me the money) one of my little boys came up to the room and said, "Mama, there is an Egyptian gentleman waiting to see you." I went down and invited him in. He had been all ready to take the train to his village, so he said, but a strong feeling came to him that he must come to the orphanage and help me before he went home. He handed me $50. I told him that it was surely God who had laid the needs of the orphanage on his heart, as we were without money and I had just gone to try to borrow some money from one of my teachers. We all got a wonderful lesson out of it.

One day I went to visit one of my Egyptian friends who was ill. I spent the day with her and she asked me how many children I had [at the orphanage]. I told her and she asked me how much money I had. I told her that I had less than $5 and that I had borrowed $250 from one of my friends. She then inquired about our new buildings saying, "Of course you don't start a building until you have some extra money on hand."

I said, "Oh, we do not wait for money. When we are quite sure that we need a new building, we start if only with fifty cents, and by the time the building is finished, it is also paid for." I told her of our large two-story building, which we built . . . for the girls—how we did not owe a cent on it.

After I had been talking a long time, telling her of how God met the needs, she said, "Well, Lillian, if I didn't know it was true, I'd say it was all lies!"

As I left that evening her husband gave me $25. The next morning $55 came from America. I paid back part of the $250 which I owed.

The next afternoon I went up to the nursery. As I looked over the babies' beds, I saw that they were very much in need of some rubber sheeting. Theirs were quite worn out. I said to one of our teachers, "Oh, if I had only about $10 now!" While I was talking, one of the girls called and said, "Mama, Mrs. D. wants to speak to you on the telephone." She was a very wealthy Egyptian widow.

The woman told me that she would like to visit the orphanage, and in a short time two cars drove up. One car was full of oranges for the children, and she gave each child one as they passed by in line. As they left she handed me $150. I went to the store and bought the oilcloth for the babies, and paid nearly all the rest of my debt.

Remembering my dear friend with whom I had spent the previous Sunday, I thought I would tell her how God was meeting the needs. So I called her on the phone and told her. She said that she had hardly been able to sleep all night. She worried about me, wondering what I was going to do to meet the needs.

The next morning brought a letter from the brother in Kansas—the one who had sent the $1,000. He enclosed another check—this one for $500. This letter was addressed to Egypt!

I again telephoned my friend. She was so delighted she could hardly wait until I had finished telling it so she could call her husband and tell him how God had met the need.

When we keep our eyes on Him, everything seems easy, oh, so easy. But when we begin to look at circumstances, we shake and tremble with fear . . . all is well, because He careth for us.

9

I FOUND
THE BEST IN LIFE

Alexander Lindsay

When I was 22, I left Scotland for the United States and soon got a job at Baldwin's Locomotive Shop in Philadelphia as a blacksmith. I felt a great urge to seek the best in life. The longing became so strong that I was desperate in my search. I left Philadelphia and went to Toronto, Canada, to a church where an evangelistic band from a college was holding meetings. I felt I had to find that obscure something, the best in life.

In that service the leader made this statement: "I would not ask any young man to become a Christian if there were anything unmanly in it or if it did not give him the best in life."

I am certain that God, in His concern for me, put those words in the minister's mouth. He went on to ask anyone who desired Jesus as Saviour to come to the altar. That was something I simply could not do. In all the years I had attended church in Scotland, we had never been asked to do any such thing, and to me it was unthinkable. I started to leave the service when a power gripped me and turned me around, leading me back into the building.

I did not kneel, however, and left the church unsatisfied. The next evening I returned to the meeting. But when the unsaved were invited to the altar, I felt that I could not go in public. Then suddenly the same power that had compelled me the night before seemed to lift me to my feet. I went forward and knelt at the altar.

My knees had barely touched the floor when a miracle happened. I knew that Christ had come into my life. I arose and faced the people and told them I could not keep my seat. I had at last found the best thing in life.

Although I had no idea at that time of being called to preach, I felt the only thing worthwhile was to tell others that Jesus had saved me, and I knew it would be my life's work. All my earthly plans and wishes disappeared like mist before the rising sun. I was never so happy.

I felt led to visit people living in the poor sections of Toronto. When the residents opened their doors, I simply told them I had come to share what Jesus had done for me. At first they would stare in amazement, but when they saw I was in earnest, most of them listened. Some asked me into their homes to tell them more. Others invited me to conduct home prayer meetings.

Later, while studying for the ministry, I received word that a peculiar sect called "holy rollers" were in the city holding meetings. Out of curiosity I went to the meetings. It was too much for my reserved nature, and I left, not expecting to return.

However, the Lord began to deal with me, and I attended another service. There for the first time in my life I had a vision of Jesus. He smiled and seemed to beckon me, as though He were saying that this was for me. He gave me a hunger to be filled with the Spirit and at the same time showed me the standard I would have to reach: a life cleansed of everything which was not of God.

I got down to business immediately and prayed the prayer

of David, "Search me, O God, and know my heart; try me, and know my thoughts: and see if there be any wicked way in me, and lead me in the way everlasting."

Instead of filling me, the Lord first emptied me—it took three days to do it. When I knelt on the third night, there was nothing between God and me. His power fell on me and knocked me to the floor. All I could do was laugh in the Spirit; then a volume of tongues came at the same time.

Up to this time I had been preparing for a ministry in another denomination and was pastoring a church of that faith. Now I felt completely out of place, for there was no liberty to preach the baptism in the Holy Spirit. I told the dean of theology of my experience and that I felt I should resign from my church. He was disturbed and told me it wasn't necessary. He only wanted me to keep quiet about the experience. He was very kind, but I had to be faithful to God at any cost. My bride and I left our friends there and launched out to see what God had for us.

My first Pentecostal church was a pioneer work where I was both pastor and janitor. The people were very poor and the congregation small, but they did the best they could to support the church. They tithed all their vegetables, milk, eggs and meat.

Our second church was also new. When my wife and I arrived in that small community in northern Canada, we knew no one and had no place to stay for the night. Having noticed an empty barn about a mile before when our train stopped at a flag station, we took our suitcases and started for it.

We knocked at the door of the farmhouse and explained who we were and why we were in the community. The farmer's wife invited us in. As we talked to her, we helped clean a large can of berries. When we were finished, she invited us to have a meeting at her house. A nice group of people came at her invitation, and we had a grand

Pentecostal meeting.

The news of people being slain under God's power spread throughout the community, and we began to hold meetings in the schoolhouse. People came from as far as twelve miles away (a long way in those days). Among those saved was one man over eighty years old. Our meeting lasted two weeks. During that time we had potatoes and cucumbers for breakfast, dinner, and supper, but in our zeal we never tired of this diet.

In 1918 the Lord called us to India, to a mission station called Rupaidiha, on the borders of Nepal. Here we saw the real India, for the people were practically untouched by western civilization. We loved this place and the people.

We had been in India barely a year when I awoke one morning with sharp cutting pains in my thigh from sciatica. The attacks were so severe I would faint from sheer pain. Our station was remote, and my wife could find nothing to relieve my pain. One of our national workers stayed by my bedside day and night, praying and doing what he could to help, but no relief came.

One day—I shall never forget it—I was suffering terribly when a heavy pressure seemed to fill my room. A voice whispered in my ear, "Go insane, and you will not feel the pain so much." I wanted to yield to the temptation, when suddenly the power of God fell upon the national worker, and he cried, "Alexander, look to the Cross!" This man was a Hindu and had no knowledge of English. It was the Spirit of the living God who spoke to me through him. The awful Satanic pressure lifted, and the room seemed filled with glory. Something like lightning flashed through my body, and the pain disappeared, never to return.

After returning from India, we pastored a number of churches in the U.S.A. I have always lived by faith and trusted God to supply my needs. *Faith is the victory!* Thank God, I found the best in life.

10

THE MINISTRY OF "BROTHER TOM"

Alice Reynolds Flower

During the outpouring of the Holy Spirit at Azusa Street Mission, Los Angeles, a Wesleyan Methodist minister, Thomas Hezmalhalch, came from Leeds, England, to receive the Pentecostal fullness which added to his already rich experience with God.

Soon after receiving the Holy Spirit, he visited Indianapolis, my early home, where Pentecostal showers were beginning to fall. Under the ministry of "Brother Tom" (as we were encouraged to address him because his name was so difficult) and his party, the moving of God's Spirit increased and copious showers of latter rain came from heaven. This is when I received the baptism in the Holy Spirit (Easter Sunday, March 21, 1907).

God actually took me by surprise the first day I attended these special meetings; but there had been a solid religious background in my own home as well as under the able ministry of Pastor and Mrs. George N. Eldridge in the Christian and Missionary Alliance church which we faithfully attended.

Dr. A.B. Simpson frequently visited our Alliance Branch, considered one of the strongest in the Midwest. On his first visit after my receiving the fullness of the Spirit, he told me he had heard of my experience, and believed, asking me to write to him all about it. This has always been a precious memory, for as a young girl I greatly revered this man of God.

To return to Brother Tom and the privilege of being under his ministry during those early days: he radiated the love of God even in the very sprightly manner in which he walked into the service. Just a fringe of white hair encircled his bald pate, and there were certain discrepancies in his teeth when he smiled; but his face actually shone with the glory of God with whom he walked continually. There was a heavenly light about his customary smile as he entered the company of believers; and we felt an immediate lift in spirit. His very presence ministered the grace so richly evident from his personal relationship with God.

Such an attitude stimulated hunger in our hearts for a similar walk with God following our baptism in the Holy Spirit. Young and old were encouraged to respond wholeheartedly to the promptings of the Spirit. Under his ministry there were no "cut and dried" meetings, as often we literally sat on the edge of our chairs, so eager were we to obey the Spirit and fit into our place in the program developed under God. Sometimes a burden of prayer caused us to drop on our knees right at our seats, quietly holding on for some special need or victory in the service. There was full liberty yet wise guidance from our brother when necessary.

Brother Tom ministered the Word in faith-quickening power; but there came to me a sense of the vital importance of responding with a childlike spontaneity to each impulse of God's hand. There were unusual meetings when God used some unlikely one to accomplish miracles in bodies as well as souls.

We were taught to court the Spirit's moving and through

the intervening years the urgency of this has greatly dominated my personal life along various lines of ministry. There were no ruts to our training, no spiritual habits; we were encouraged to expect a fresh working of God in any service, noting whichever direction the heavenly winds blew and learning to trim our sails accordingly.

Just a week after receiving the Comforter I had my first experience of singing in the heavenly choir. A brother was testifying at some length when Brother Tom interrupted him: "Hold on, brother; God is seeking to move in our midst." The brother stopped, then continued. Again Brother Tom checked him, kindly but firmly. Then we heard it—a low humming that gradually rose in harmonious crescendo as six individuals in different parts of the audience rose spontaneously to their feet and a full tide of glorious melody poured forth in ecstatic worship and praise.

Having been one of that group I can still feel the thrill as, for the first time, from my innermost being heavenly music poured forth like strains through the pipes of some great organ. No effort, no self-consciousness—just the flowing forth of celestial harmony like a foretaste of divine rapture. Thanks be to God for the many times this holy joy has been repeated. Brother Tom had sensed God's desire and simply made room for His working.

Often I have thanked God for the example, the precepts of Brother Tom in my early years of Pentecostal living and practice. He has been in glory these many years, but his godly influence lives on in my life and others who knew him.

When God takes over, what marvelous refreshing and divine accomplishment comes to His people in mere moments of time. No wonder we cry out in these days of increasing formality and often times too rigid organization, "Oh, that thou wouldest rend the heavens: that thou wouldest come down that the mountains might flow down at thy presence" (Isaiah 64:1,2).

11

RAYMOND T. RICHEY, GOD'S PINCH HITTER

Eloise May Richey

In October 1920 Warren Collins was to begin a meeting in Hattiesburg, Mississippi. Raymond T. Richey (who later became my husband) promised to assist him. Raymond went a week or so early to make arrangements and to advertise the meeting. The building was rented, hotel reservations were made, and advertising put out for Warren Collins to begin preaching on a certain day.

Then came a telegram from Collins saying that it was impossible for him to come.

There was Raymond in a strange place, among strange people, all arrangements made for the meeting, and a wire from the evangelist saying that he would not be there. He was certainly at the end of his resources.

Then God spoke to him and told him to go ahead and conduct the meeting himself. But he would not listen to the Lord. The committee that had secured the first evangelist advised him to go home, and they would help him pay the bills. But Raymond could not get the consent of his own heart to leave.

Finally he locked himself in his hotel room. For three days

and three nights he fasted and prayed that God should make His will so plain to him that there could be no doubt and no hesitation in his own heart as to just what God would have him do.

At the end of those three days, with no money at all and with no cooperation—not even from the committee that had invited Collins—he left his room, went to the newspaper office and placed an ad stating that on Thursday he would begin "An Old-Time Revival and Gospel of Healing Meeting" in the Red Circle Auditorium. On that evening the revival began.

About fifteen people were there. They came with an air of "What do you expect?" But Raymond refused to be discouraged. He gave a short talk on the need of revival and what would be required to bring one. . . . The next evening it rained, but there were thirty or forty present. But on the third night the sick were prayed for. The first person to be prayed for was a young lady with a crooked arm. The doctors had done everything possible, even trying to straighten it with some kind of mechanical device. Raymond prayed for her, and instantly that arm was straightened. This was written up in the newspaper the following day. That evening the building was filled.

In three weeks of meetings, God saved hundreds of souls and hundreds were prayed for for healing.

The Rev. Arch P. Collins of Fort Worth was a great inspiration to Raymond. For some time he was very closely associated with Raymond in the ministry, and it was Brother Collins who taught him the great secret of waiting upon God.

After the Hattiesburg meeting, Andrew Richey and his wife Anna (Raymond's brother and sister-in-law) joined the party. They too had experienced marvelous healings. Anna in fact had been raised from her deathbed.

Campaigns were held in various cities in Mississippi. One afternoon while in Laurel, Mississippi, as we were praying, an awful burden for Houston, Texas, (our home city) seized Raymond and then Anna. We prayed and wept before the Lord, and He made it clear that we were to go to Houston and launch a campaign. It was not to be just a revival meeting in a church but a great city-wide interdenominational campaign where thousands could be reached with the gospel of Christ.

When we reached home, we talked with some of the loved ones about it, but they were a bit fearful for us. Such a meeting would require thousands of dollars and would necessitate numbers of trained workers. We did not have the money, and we did not know where to secure the workers. However, so sure were Raymond and Andrew that it was the voice of God that they secured a large tent seating about a thousand, rented a piano, built seats, arranged for lights, and launched the campaign.

The first night a soldier boy was saved; a few nights later he was prayed for and healed and was soon discharged from the army hospital. Crowds began to come. Soon all the seats were filled, and people were standing around the tent trying to see and hear. Raymond announced that if money could be raised to pay the rent in the city auditorium, we would go down there. In just a few minutes' time the money was raised.

For forty nights this revival continued and increased in attendance and interest and in conversions and healings. Night after night the city auditorium seating many thousands were filled. At times even standing room was a premium. God gave us five thousand conversions in this meeting and some of the most marvelous miracles of healing I have ever witnessed.

One morning it had been announced that there would be a

special service for those who had to be brought in on cots and wheelchairs—there were thirteen carried in on stretchers from ambulances besides those who had come in wheelchairs. After the message and the great altar service where hundreds found Christ in salvation, these thirteen were prayed for, and twelve of them were healed and able to go home either on the street cars or in automobiles of their friends. Only one returned home in an ambulance.

Thus began a series of campaigns which took the Richey party across America and into the cities of the Caribbean. It only goes to show what God can do with a yielded life—in this case, Raymond T. Richey, in a hotel room in Hattiesburg, Mississippi.

12

THE MULTIPLYING OF THE BREAD

Oskar Jeske

When God sends a revival, it is often accompanied by supernatural acts that amaze even hardened unbelievers. I witnessed such a miracle when I was a fourteen-year-old boy in Poland.

During the summer of 1916 a great revival swept our area, and newly converted Christians traveled to various meeting places and ministered. One such zealous group was under the leadership of a devout school teacher, a Mr. Drews.

Drews started a choir in the Vistula lowlands area in the Gostynin district, and he promised that he would bring the choir to our services in the German village of Grabie. We eagerly awaited their visit.

One Sunday afternoon I saw two farm carts approaching our house. I told my mother and when she learned that it was Mr. Drews and his singers, she panicked. It was wartime, everything was rationed, and mother had no bread to feed the seventeen people. Because the meeting was to begin at three and it was now long past dinnertime, there was no time to cook anything.

After the greetings were over, Mother sent me to our

next-door neighbor to borrow some bread while she busied herself in the kitchen preparing something to eat. In no time I was back but with no bread. The neighbors had no bread and would not be baking until the next day. Mother sent me to another neighbor, but again I returned without bread. Then she asked me to go to our Polish neighbors, but I knew they had eaten the last of their bread on the previous evening.

Mother stood perplexed. "What shall I do, Oskar?" Slowly she went to the cupboard and took out a square piece of bread which may have weighed about a pound and held it in her hands.

I looked at the bread, then at her. "Mamma," I said, "if Jesus were here, He would take the piece of bread out of your hand, bless it, and then give it back to you and say, 'Cut it. There will be enough for all and more.' "

Mother put her arms around me and with tears in her eyes kissed me. "Cut as much as you have, Mamma," I said, "and tell our friends that there is a war on. Everyone is to take a small piece as far as it lasts; they will understand."

I went back to talk with the choir members. . . . After some time I decided to return to the kitchen to see how Mother was making out.

I stared in astonishment. There in the middle of the kitchen table stood a plate piled high with bread, and a second plate was already half filled. "Mamma," I gasped, "where did you get all that bread?"

My mother, startled, let the knife fall from her hand. In her other hand she still held the small piece of bread from which she had started cutting. Yet the piece had not become much smaller than when she had begun. Trembling, she answered, "Oh, praise God! Jesus has blessed the bread."

She took the bread to a table that had been set up and prepared the rest of the meal. Then seventeen guests,

Grandfather, my aunt, Mother, and I all sat down at the table and began to eat. We ate our fill, yet there was still a great deal of bread left. Mother urged the guests to eat more. When everyone had finished, she asked, "Do you know what sort of bread we have eaten?"

"Yes," Mr. Drews answered, "rye bread; and very good, too."

"Yes," Mother replied, "and you have eaten bread blessed by Jesus." Then she told the story. Everyone began to praise God; some began to weep. Still praising God, we went to the meeting where Mr. Drews preached a powerful sermon. Christians consecrated themselves anew and sinners were persuaded to surrender themselves to the Lord.

Late that night when the meeting finally ended, the guests and Mother and I were invited to the home of a rich farmer's wife who was also a Christian. The table was filled with wonderful things to eat. When everyone was seated, a woman mentioned the miracle that happened in our kitchen. All were so filled with praise and thanks that they forgot the meal and knelt for several hours, praising God.

Shortly before daybreak, after again praying together, these brothers and sisters in Christ started joyfully on their way home.

I'll never forget the multiplying of the bread—the first miracle that I had ever seen.

13

MY PERSONAL EXPERIENCE AT THE AZUSA MISSION

Ernest S. Williams

In August, 1906 a young friend and I were in the state of Colorado when we received letters telling of the outpouring of the Holy Spirit in Los Angeles. In September we went to Los Angeles, our home city, to see for ourselves what was happening.

My first visit to the Azusa Street Mission was on a Sunday morning. There I saw what I had never seen before. Although there was considerable inspiration in the meeting it was the altar service at the conclusion that fascinated me. The front of the mission was packed with seekers and persons trying to assist them. Christians and unsaved spectators crowded around to see what was going on. Some at the altar were seeking to be filled with the Holy Spirit; others were worshiping God in unknown tongues. I looked on not knowing what to think. My heart was hungry for God. I knew God in the salvation of my soul, but was not satisfied. Were it not for the unsatisfied hunger I might have turned away, for I had been taught that entire sanctification and the baptism with the Holy Spirit were one. We called this the second blessing, conversion being the first. I began to read my Bible to see if it taught a third blessing.

On the brink of turning away, a great check came over my spirit and I felt that by resisting I was rejecting God. Then I began to seek earnestly.

In my first seeking I was not praying that I might be filled with the Spirit, but asking God if there was anything in my life that was not what He would have it be, or that was not given up to His will. Finding no condemnation, I began to seek the baptism with the Spirit and on October 2, I received.

I had some wonderful experiences while I was seeking the Lord. The greatest, perhaps, came one week before I spoke in other tongues. I had tarried at the altar that night until all but two other persons were gone. It seemed that as I worshiped, God was taking hold of my flesh, not in physical manifestation, but in divine penetration. With it came such rest that I felt I could have remained at that altar the rest of my life.

At midnight I stood and said, "I have gotten something; what is it?" I was told, "You have received the anointing." That was all right with me, though I did not know what to name it. From that time until I reached the climax of my experience a week later, I walked in undisturbed and spiritual peace, feeling as though I were protected from any invasion by hills of God on either side.

This was my introduction into the Pentecostal Movement. A Holiness friend warned me that I had gotten into error and would soon find it out. Over seventy years have passed since then and I am still in the Pentecostal Movement, looking for the Lord to come to take His people home and, should He tarry, to be transported by the angels of God in the hour of death to be forever with the Lord.

14

PERSONAL EXPERIENCES OF DIVINE HEALING

P.S. Jones

In 1925, in the city of Victoria, British Columbia, the Lord Jesus baptized me in the Holy Spirit, according to Acts 2:4. My knowledge of Bible truths was very limited, and I had to search the Scriptures for confirmation that all was well. I found it was, and have rejoiced in this life in the Spirit ever since.

I was a diabetic and had been placed on a strict diet. About that time a man of God, who had been marvelously healed under the ministry of Dr. Charles S. Price, befriended me. Lovingly and intelligently he introduced me to the truth of divine healing. This was quite foreign to me, for before this time I had placed my whole confidence in doctors and their prescriptions. My friend's explanations took root in my unclouded soul, and no doctrinal prejudice interfered with the growth of faith. One day I said to him, "I am going to get my healing." I did not understand the implications of this stand, but I meant it as far as I knew.

One evening I went to a Presbyterian church and was prayed for by the minister, who believed in divine healing. God's power was evident when he laid his hands on my head and prayed the prayer of faith.

The next day, as I sat at the dinner table and faced my diet menu, a strong conviction came to me that if I believed God had healed me I should not diet any longer. So in simplicity of faith I set aside the diet and from then on ate normally what was set before me, giving thanks to God.

From that time on I forgot I had been a diabetic and for many years had no physical examination. The desire for very sweet food was taken from me.

While in Calgary, Alberta, I needed auto insurance, and a medical certificate was required. I went to a doctor for examination. One of the questions to be answered was, "Is he a diabetic?" The doctor wrote "No." To God be the glory!

Later I was hospitalized and again a strict examination revealed there was no trace of diabetes.

At the time I was first prayed for, I was also afflicted with chronic appendicitis. Every few weeks I had attacks of abdominal pains and could not eat until the pains subsided. After I was prayed for the symptoms returned only once. They continued for several hours. They bothered me during the night, but the Lord gave me sleep, and when I awakened for the third time the pains had disappeared.

As I was about to take a cold bath in the morning, the enemy challenged me to take no risks after such inflammation, but I took my stand in the Lord, saying, "Satan, if you are stronger than Jesus, you win; but He is stronger than you." After that there was no more trouble. Praise the Lord!

I also had a painful rectal condition which doctors told me could only be relieved by an operation. After I took my stand in Christ, several weeks of severe testing followed. Once when tortured with pain I gritted my teeth and shouted, "Lord, I do believe."

Suddenly I heard the voice of the Spirit in my soul saying,

"What are you doing?"

I said, "Lord, I am trying to believe you."

Then came the words never to be forgotten, "Well, stop trying and believe Me."

"All right, Lord," I said. "I don't understand what you mean, but I'll do it anyway." So from that time I rested my case, literally doing nothing to "try to believe." Thanks be to God, in a few weeks the Lord healed that which the doctors said could not be put right without surgery.

What the Lord said to Israel was true: "I am the Lord that healeth thee" (Exodus 15:26).

15

WHEN GOD VISITS ST. LOUIS

Mary Woodworth-Etter

The Lord was calling me to St. Louis, Missouri, April 1890, but I wanted to stay in California through the summer. I had quite a struggle, not knowing just what to do. I placed my goods on the train and made plans to go to Los Angeles. That night I received a letter inviting me to St. Louis, so I sold our household goods and started the next morning for St. Louis.

Nobody knew our little band of workers was coming until our meeting was announced. The first night eighteen were present. God was there in power. Two were converted. The crowds grew larger every day, and souls were converted at every meeting. A number of remarkable cases of divine healing were wrought by the Lord.

One Sunday afternoon we were invited to hold a meeting in the Union Market. We felt the Lord was leading in thi and accepted the invitation. We had a large, attentive congregation. The streetcars were passing by loaded with people who wanted to see the new bridge that had just been built across the Mississippi River.

It was now the first of June, and we were ready to put up

our large tent, which we brought from California. The only place we could get room enough was "Kerry Patch," a place noted for the hoodlum element. People had been shot, robbed, and stoned there any hour of the day.

The Christians tried to persuade us not to pitch our tents in "Kerry Patch," and after we had them up these good folks urged us to move away from the wicked and rough element, but we felt God had led us there. The Christians told us that several show tents put up where ours stood had been torn down. They argued that if the rough element would cut the ropes of a show tent, surely a gospel tent would have little chance to stand. We answered that God had placed us there and by His grace we would stay.

Many of our best friends were afraid to let their wives and daughters come, and they felt they were running a great risk in coming themselves, because the congregation was stoned coming and going. Sometimes the stones went flying through the tent.

Most of the people in the area had never been inside a church. They did not know what a campmeeting was, thinking it was some kind of a show.

The first night the tent—which seated eight thousand—was crowded. Men stood on the seats with hats on, cigars and pipes in their mouths, coats off and sleeves rolled up. Women with old dirty aprons and dresses, bare-headed, and bare-armed were there. Some of the people would shoot off firecrackers. When we sang, they sang louder. When we prayed, they clapped their hands and cheered us. They were armed with pistols and clubs and were ready to kill us and tear down the tent. It looked as if we would all be killed. Several ministers tried to talk, but they were stoned down or their voices drowned out. It looked like surrender or death.

It was an awful sight to see a little band of Christians

sitting nearly frozen to their seats with fear and surrounded by a mob of wild, fierce men and women, many of whom were half drunk and their eyes and faces red and inflamed. Every effort failed and we could do nothing with them. I said to my co-workers: "We will never give up, and if they take us out of the tent before we are ready to go, they will take us out dead." I told them to lead in prayer one after the other and the God of Elijah would answer.

A woman knelt at the pulpit pale as death, her hands and face raised to heaven, and in a clear ringing voice asked God to save and bless the judgment-bound crowd. A feeling of the awful presence of God began to fall on the people. Another woman followed in prayer. Then I arose and stood before them.

I raised my hand in the name of the Lord and commanded them to listen. The Lord had sent me there to do them good, I told them, and I would not leave until the Lord told me to—when our work was done. I told them the Lord would strike dead the first one who tried to harm us or strike us with a dagger. The power of God fell, and the fear of God came upon the multitude. Sweat came on their faces, and they stood as though in a trance. The men began to take their pipes and cigars from their mouths and their hats from their heads. The women began to cover up their necks and arms with their aprons. They felt they stood naked and guilty before God. They began to get off the seats and sit down, but some fell and lay as dead. Others stood with their mouths open. Tears ran down their faces, leaving streaks through the dirt. They stood as though they were afraid to move. Then they all quietly moved out of the tent.

The hoodlum element always respected me after that meeting. Many would take off their hats when they passed me, but they stoned the believers coming and going to the meetings. And they threw stones through and over the tent for some time.

Finally, with the kindness of the police and the power of God, the hoodlums were driven away. The rest quieted down. Then the civilized people came when the situation was under control. We do not blame the people for being afraid. It was only by the grace of God we stood through the showers of stones. Some of the worst characters on earth came to the meeting to cause trouble. If God had not protected us we would not have left that campground alive. Glory to God! He never leaves His children.

The women and children began to wear cleaner clothes. They wore bonnets and left their dirty aprons at home. The men shaved and combed and came with their families. They said the meeting was doing good, that their wives and children were getting more tidy and keeping their homes cleaner. I told those who opposed the meeting that if it did no good except to clean up some of their citizens and better their moral condition, that it was a good work and they ought to give us a helping hand. Many of the best citizens came to the meeting and were astonished at the great victory we had gained over the rough element.

We had six small tents besides the large one, and it looked like a little town. We no longer feared for our lives and slept in our tents with our workers like little babes. Oh, praise the Lord for His care and protection!

For five months the meeting continued—night and day. The tent held eight thousand and outside were thousands more. Many sick people were carried in and got up and walked out. The blind shouted for joy, the lame threw away their crutches, the deaf and dumb clapped their hands while tears of joy ran down their faces. Children who had never walked ran about praising the Lord. Some, both young and old who were perfectly helpless, received shocks from heaven's battery that sent life through their limbs. They clapped their hands and jumped and cried for joy.

The fear of God continued to sweep over the congregation; some ran after those who were healed; others stood pale as death, looking for them to fly away, or fall dead. But when they saw that the sick were really healed, the fear of God gripped them, and they said, "We have seen strange things today."

Hundreds of men, women, and children—of all classes—were struck down by the power of God and lay as dead, some for hours and some for days. But all came out shouting the high praises of God. Many had wonderful visions of heaven and future events.

Many of the people were baptized in the Holy Spirit and received gifts. They spoke in other languages as the Spirit gave them utterance. This was nothing new to me as people have spoken in tongues throughout my ministry.

I laid hands on a young lady and prayed for her. She fell under the power and received the baptism in the Holy Spirit. She spoke several different languages fluently and with great power, and she also received the gift of interpretation and could read and write the language. A returned missionary from South Africa said one of the languages was one that was spoken by a tribe he had been working among.

The young woman later went to Europe and then to Jerusalem. On the way she stopped at the Pittsburgh Missionary Home. Some returned missionaries said the young woman talked with more power and understood the language better than those who had learned it while on the field. This is, as far as we knew, the first person sent out qualified by the Holy Spirit to preach in a language she had never learned.

One day a helpless little girl was brought to me. She could neither talk nor walk. After I prayed for her, I told some of the folks to take her out and let her try to walk. . . . After a while they brought her back. She was walking and talking, but they could not understand a word she said! Praise the Lord! She had the use of her whole body; she was walking, and talking in a strange language or tongue. She was filled with the Spirit and was as bold as a lion.

I stood her on the platform, and she began to walk about and preach. With hands uplifted . . . she preached to the astonished multitude, showing what great things the Lord had done for her.

People said it was the greatest battle ever fought in the Mississippi Valley—a battle of religion against science, the works of man, and the powers of darkness. The whole city was shaken. Missions started in many places. The churches began to have street meetings, and to visit the prisons and hospitals as they had never done before.

The people told us we would never stay three months and that we would lose the rent money. But, praise God, we stayed the three months and then engaged the ground for two months more!

The man who owned the ground was a Catholic. He was so pleased with the change in the neighborhood for good, he said he would let us have the ground free of charge. The interest in the meeting was widespread—reaching from the Atlantic to the Pacific and across the ocean. I received letters from prominent ministers in Canada and all parts of the country inquiring about the great work God was doing in St. Louis. People came two thousand miles to be saved or to have their bodies healed. Some of the physicians said they knew there had been six hundred persons healed. They said many of these had been given up by the best physicians of St. Louis. It was true that thousands were saved, hundreds healed—and many were saved and healed at the same time. . . . Several children who had never walked were healed.

Those who had been deaf all their lives had their hearing restored perfectly. Many had their sight restored. Some who were dumb were made to speak. Many infants were healed of all kinds of afflictions. Some who were brought on beds walked away. Many were made to stretch out their withered arms. The paralytic got up and walked.

While holding this meeting, a boy was brought to us who had been caught and thrown into a dog wagon by the dog catchers and frightened nearly to death. He went mad, and would have awful mad spells, or fits, every night or day for a period of two years. All that medical skill could do had been done, but to no avail.

It was a peculiar case. The mother told me that doctors from Germany had tried to cure him but all had failed and that all hopes of ever doing so were given up. At times he was all right. He heard about the meetings and begged his mother to take him.

She brought him one Sunday. She had him in the great crowd near the outer edge of the camp when he took one of his mad spells and began snapping and biting at everyone. The people were panic stricken, so they took him to my small tent. There he caught hold of the heavy canvas with his teeth and bit and chewed a hole in it—several inches each way. Hundreds saw all of this.

I told the boy's mother never to bring him back, for we would be arrested. But he was better after that and begged his mother to take him back to the meetings. One night (as I was working at the long altar and preaching to hundreds) the mother and her boy stood by my side. I was so scared; but I saw how much faith she had.

And the boy looked so pitiful that the Lord gave me faith to pray for him. He was completely healed.

Nearly the whole city knew about the boy's condition; and when they heard that he was healed, and his mind perfectly restored, they all wanted to see him. I would ask him to come up on the big platform, and he would step out so manly, and tell that the Lord had saved, and healed him, and had filled him with His Spirit.

For years after, when I went to the city every Sunday, he would come walking down the aisle to the pulpit, with a lovely bouquet of flowers.

The mouths of the gainsayers, scoffers, and liars were stopped. Thousands of souls were saved. Several police, many Catholics, many Germans and people of other nations were represented at the altar, weeping their way to Calvary.

When the weather became too cold for our tents, we rented a church building down in the best part of the city. We started a mission of over four hundred members. The interest of the meetings had continued to increase all summer, and when we went into the church God was there in mighty power, with signs and wonders following.

16

IT TOOK A MIRACLE

Glenn Renick

It was a cold day in January 1928 when I started for Hannibal, Missouri, behind the wheel of an old Model T Ford. The car had no heat, and the flapping curtains assured the driver of plenty of fresh air.

I made the trip in relays from one store to another along the highway, stopping at each to warm by a friendly stove, as was common in those days.

Such a trip usually provided one incident to be remembered, and this was no exception. The thud, thud, of a rear wheel signaled trouble somewhere between two stores, and there was nothing to do but jack up the car and remove the wheel. I found the brake shoe ruined and only one lug left in the hub.

Only one familiar with wooden spokes and wheels can appreciate the problem that faced this young preacher—his trip half over and him nearly frozen. But the prayer of faith was answered, and I arrived at my destination on a prayer and a wheel with one lug holding.

Two Christians living on a farm near Hannibal had rented an old store building on North Main Street and invited us to come and start meetings. The building boasted one stove with pipes, supported by wires, running the length of the building. Once the pipe broke, and what a mess! Soot, smoke, and even fire billowed from the open pipe—a common incident for a pioneer preacher.

A platform of tile and planks, seats from an old tent, and a rug for the altar area completed the furnishings. With two months rent paid by our friends, we were on our own. It was just God and I. It took a miracle to pioneer a church in those days. The preacher lived by faith and had few material blessings; but when he was sure of his call, believed in his God and acted accordingly, God honored the sacrifice and gave the increase.

The revival meeting started on January 25. Thirty-five people came to the altar and professed salvation in the first meeting, and many who were bound with evil habits testified of deliverance. Threats were made against me, but I suffered no bodily harm.

Later we moved into a small dwelling converted into a church. The pulpit and altar were in the center, allowing the speaker to look into two rooms. In this humble place God worked miracles of healing and deliverance. Let me tell you about one.

Mrs. Crawford Adams was afflicted with a toxic goiter and had a rapid heartbeat. She often fainted and lay unconscious. One night she asked her husband, who was not a believer, if she might go forward and ask for prayer. He consented, and she was anointed and prayed for. Then it seemed as if she fainted and she appeared to be in a coma.

Her husband was concerned, and so were we. While we wondered what to do, she slowly lifted her hand. Color came back into her face, and she began to speak in the most beautiful language. The place was electrified. This Baptist woman received the baptism in the Holy Spirit and healing for her body at the same time. The place was charged with the power of God. It was a miracle, visible to all.

She testified, "When I was anointed with oil and hands were laid upon me, I felt the power of God strike me, and it seemed as though crystal-clear water flowed through my body, beginning at my head. The same power reversed itself and came through my body again, beginning at my feet. When it reached my throat, I felt something snap. My heartbeat became normal. I was healed."

This healing turned the tide in Hannibal. It was widely known and much discussed. We were able to move the services from the house to a vacant downtown theater. The press and radio became friendly, and doors were opened to us where we least expected it. This miracle of healing came through the mighty power of God in answer to travailing prayer. The same God still answers prayer today when we believe and act upon our faith.

17

AN OUTSTANDING HEALING IN TORONTO

Mrs. George L. Flower

John Easton had a broken back and for six years had lived in a plaster cast with a harness on his shoulders from which weights were suspended—sleeping in a wagon from which during the daytime he sold small items—pencils, tablets, songsheets, oranges, etc.—on the streets of Toronto. At night he drove his horse and wagon into a barn, the loft of which was finished for his wife and children to occupy. His legs were so dead that a needle could be stuck into the flesh without any resultant feeling. His heels were drawn up until the feet were straight with the legs, so that there was no possibility of his walking. The occasional changing of his cast necessitated his being suspended by cords lest his vertebrae make such contact that he would be thrown into convulsions.

My husband and I attended the meetings held in his barn on Friday nights week after week as instruction on salvation and healing was given to the man. But I missed the final meeting when John Easton was healed. . . . My husband was there, however, and saw the miracle performed. That very day John Easton received from God assurance of healing. He told his wife to purchase proper clothes and shoes for him and her hesitancy because of fear did not daunt him in the least.

There was a feeling of expectancy in the meeting from the start until the actual moment when the leader with the help of others sawed the cast open.

At the command "In the name of Jesus," John Easton sat up! His feet and legs hung over the sides of the wagon like two sacks. At a second word of command, he lowered himself upon his feet and those feet became normal immediately. He picked the leader up in his arms, then turned to embrace his wife.

Hearing the sound of rejoicing, the neighbors and then the newsmen began coming in. All night he walked and praised the Lord until by morning the soft flesh of his "new" feet was blistered. But he was in church the next Sunday, giving his marvelous testimony to an overflowing house. It was a witness through Toronto which none could gainsay.

Editor's Note: This story is from *Grandmother Flower's Story,* p. 4, by Mrs. George L. Flower. The story was reported in the Toronto Ontario *Evening Telegram,* Saturday, February 15, 1902, and in *Leaves of Healing,* August 2, 1902, edited by John Alexander Dowie, Zion, Illinois.

18

MEMOIRS OF THE
AZUSA REVIVAL

Frank Bartleman

I went to Burbank Hall, Sunday morning, April 15, 1906. A colored sister was there and spoke in tongues. This created quite a stir. The people gathered in little companies on the sidewalk after the service, inquiring what this might mean. We learned that the Holy Spirit had fallen a few nights before on April 9 at a little cottage on Bonnie Brae Street. They had been tarrying very earnestly for some time for an outpouring of the Holy Ghost.

For some reason I was not privileged to be present in that particular meeting. I went to the Bonnie Brae meeting in the afternoon and found God working mightily. We had been praying for many months for victory; the pioneers had broken through and the multitudes were to follow.

There was a general spirit of humility manifested in the meeting. They were taken up with God. Evidently the Lord had found the little company at last through whom He could have right of way. Others were in the hands of men, and the Holy Spirit could not work. Others far more pretentious had failed. That which man esteems had been passed by once more, the Holy Spirit choosing a humble "stable" outside ecclesiastical establishments.

The meeting was moved to 312 Azusa Street. They had cleared enough space to lay some planks on top of empty nail kegs, with seats enough for possibly thirty people. These were arranged in a square, facing one another. On my first visit to Azusa, I found about a dozen saints there. Brother Seymour was in charge. The "ark of God" moved off slowly but surely. It was carried on "the shoulders" of His own appointed priests at the beginning. The "priests" were alive unto God through much preparation and prayer. It was not all blessing. In fact the fight was terrific. But the fire could not be smothered. Strong saints gathered together in prayer and gradually the tide rose in victory. A small beginning, and a very small flame.

I gave a message at my first meeting at Azusa. Two of the saints spoke in tongues. It was soon noised abroad that God was working at Azusa. All classes began to flock to the meetings. Many were curious and unbelieving, but others were hungry for God. The newspapers began to ridicule and abuse the meetings, thus giving us much free advertising, and bringing crowds. The devil overdid himself. Outside persecution never hurt the work; we had the most to fear from the working of evil spirits within. Even spiritualists and hypnotists came to investigate and try their influence. Religious crooks and cranks came seeking a place in the work. This is always a danger to every new work. This condition threw a fear over many that was hard to overcome.

We found early in the Azusa work that when we attempted to steady the ark, the Lord stopped working. We dared not call attention of the people too much to the working of the devil. Fear would follow, but God gave the victory. Through prayer, the presence of the Lord was with us. The leaders had limited experience, and the wonder is that the work survived at all against its powerful adversaries. But it was of

God; that was the secret.

The San Francisco earthquake was surely the voice of God to the people of the Pacific Coast. It was used mightily in conviction for the gracious after-revival. In the early Azusa days both heaven and hell seemed to have come down. Men were at the breaking point. Conviction was upon the people. When men came within two or three blocks of the place, they were seized with conviction.

The work was getting clearer and stronger at Azusa. God was working and it seemed that everyone had to go there. Missionaries were gathered there from Africa, India, and the islands of the sea. Preachers and workers crossed the continent and came from distant islands with an irresistible drawing to Los Angeles. It was God's call. Holiness meetings, tents, and missions began to close up for lack of attendance. Their people were at Azusa.

There was much persecution, especially from the press. They wrote us up shamefully, but this only drew the crowds. Some gave the work six months to live. Soon the meetings were running day and night. The place was packed out nightly. The whole building upstairs and down had now been cleared and put to use. Great emphasis was placed on the blood for cleansing. A high standard was held up for a clean life. "When the enemy shall come in like a flood, the Spirit of the Lord shall lift up a standard against him" (Isa. 59:19).

Divine love was wonderfully manifest in the meetings. They would not even allow an unkind word said against their opposers in the churches. The message was the love of God. It was a return to the "first love" of the church. The Holy Spirit baptism as we received it in the beginning did not allow us to think, speak, or hear evil of any man. The Spirit was very sensitive, tender as a dove. The Holy Spirit is symbolized as a dove, and we knew the moment we had grieved the Holy Spirit by an unkind thought or deed. We seemed to live in a sea of pure divine love. The Lord fought our battles for us in those days. We committed ourselves to His judgments fully in all matters, never seeking to defend the work or ourselves. We lived in His wonderful immediate presence. And nothing contrary to His pure Spirit was allowed there.

The false was sifted out from the real by the Spirit of God. The word of God itself decided absolutely all issues.

We had no pope or hierarchy. We were brethren. We had not even a platform or pulpit in the beginning. All were on a level. The ministers were servants according to the true meaning of the Word. We did not honor men from their advantage in means or education but rather for their God-given gifts. He set the members in one body.

God broke strong men and women to pieces and put them together again for His glory. It was a tremendous overhauling process. Pride, self-assertion, self-importance, and self-esteem could not survive there.

No subjects or sermons were announced ahead of time, and there were no special speakers for such an hour. No one knew what might be coming or what God would do. We wanted to hear from God through whomever He might speak. The rich and the educated were the same as the poor and ignorant, but they found a much harder death to die. We only recognized God. No flesh might glory in His presence. They were Holy Ghost meetings led of the Lord. It had to start in poor surroundings to keep out the selfish human element. All came down in humility together at His feet. There was no pride there. The services ran almost continuously. Seeking souls could be found under the power almost any hour night and day. The place was never closed or empty. God was always there.

When we first reached the meeting, we avoided as much

as possible human contact and greeting. We wanted to meet God first. The meetings started themselves spontaneously in testimony and worship. We had no prearranged programs to be jammed through on time. Our time was the Lord's. We had real testimonies from fresh heart-experiences. A dozen people might be on their feet at one time trembling under the mighty power of God.

Presumptuous men would sometimes come among us. Especially preachers with their self-opinions. But their efforts were short-lived. They generally bit the dust in humility going through the process we had all gone through. In other words, they died out, came to see themselves in all their weakness, then in childlike humility and confession were taken up of God and transformed through the mighty baptism of the Holy Spirit.

We saw some wonderful things in those days. . . . As I wrote in Way of Faith, August 1, 1906:

"Pentecost has come to Los Angeles, the American Jerusalem. Every sect, creed and doctrine under Heaven is found in Los Angeles, as well as every nation represented. Many times I have been tempted to wonder if my strength would hold out to see it (the Pentecostal revival). The burden of prayer has been very great. But since the spring of 1905, when I first received this vision and burden, I have never doubted the final outcome of it. . . . A cleansing stream is flowing through the city. The Word of God prevails."

19

I'M GLAD I OBEYED
THE LORD

J.K. Gressett

The Lord has a plan for our lives, and it is so beautiful when we find that plan and follow it.

Shortly after I was saved and healed, the Lord began to deal with me in a strange way. I would awaken in the night crying. I would attempt to offer thanks at the table and leave crying. I cried until I couldn't see how to plow in the field.

We had no pastor to guide us in such crisis spots in those early days, so I went to the woods and told the Lord I was staying there till He helped me overcome this problem. He reminded me of the consecration I had made when I was dying. He showed me His will and became more real to me than any earthly being has ever been.

From then on my testimonies in the cottage prayer meetings grew longer—till friends said I almost preached. There was such a desire to do something for the Lord, we would drive twenty miles in a buggy to help in a revival.

The girl friend I had before I was saved would have nothing to do with me now. She couldn't enjoy my crying and going to church so much, and I surely couldn't go with her to the dances. We had been warned not to keep company with unsaved young people, and she started going with someone else. It seemed our case was about hopeless. But her sister was saved and she persuaded her to go to the prayer meeting to play the old pump organ.

One night during the song service the glory of the Lord came down. My former girl friend fell off the organ stool onto the floor. She was one of several who were saved and received the baptism in the Spirit that night.

Her boyfriend was quite provoked! The next Saturday night he went to a dance, and she came to the prayer meeting with her sister. I took her home. That was forty-eight years ago, and I still take her home. It was as simple as that. Our Lord will fix things if we will let Him.

We were married, both knowing we were to work for the Lord in some way. With scarcely any education, no pastor to guide me, and no chance to go to a Bible school, I would have enjoyed the assurance that I was to be a water boy to a good preacher.

We made a lot of beautiful plans. I rented a farm; we were going to get a car and a lot of clothes. Someday, when we got everything we needed, we would work for the Lord.

Then the house burned, with wedding gifts, wedding clothes, everything. Three days later a call came for us to help in another revival. We told loved ones good-bye, took all we had in one suitcase, and started out as if we were going to the other side of the world.

We assisted in several revivals in small western Texas oil towns. We held meetings in schoolhouses, store buildings, courthouses, abandoned churches, and in the open air. One good meeting was held in a cotton gin lot. Many were saved and filled with the Spirit. I remember a time when we lived for over a week on rice and jack rabbits that I killed. Such hardships are bright spots in our memories now.

While I was living so close to the Lord in those meetings,

He began to deal with me about the host of unsaved relatives I had left behind. I reminded Him that they forsook me first. When I was sick, they didn't visit me; and when I was saved and healed, I promised the Lord I would stay away from them if He would just bless me. (It is amazing how unsanctified we can be and still have His blessings!)

It had been three years since I had seen them, and I had no intention of ever going back. But misery has no bounds when we leave the Lord out of our plans. I felt worse than I had before I was saved. Finally I prayed through enough to tell the Lord I would go for Him, since He had been so good to me. At the same time, I tried to convince Him with what I knew about them that it was a lost cause.

The way opened up in three days after I became willing to go, and our party of five was transported three hundred miles without a penny's cost.

When I told my two uncles we were there for a meeting, they said they had heard we were crazy and now they believed it. It was April. There we were ten miles from town, uninvited, unwelcome, at a crossroads where people had no interest in religion. Three halfhearted sinner farmers helped us build a brush arbor and roll logs in place for seats.

For three full weeks we preached without apparent results. At the end we agreed to close that night if no break came. I reminded the Lord it really did look like a lost cause.

That was the night the Lord came down. Twenty-two people of all ages came to the altar. When a count was taken at three o'clock in the morning, eleven had been filled with the Spirit and several saved. There had also been some marvelous healings.

As those meetings progressed, the people began to come early to pray. We had grove meetings—the men would go one way in the woods to pray, and the women another. There were times when people would be receiving the baptism in both grove meetings and in the arbor at the same time.

People came for miles. The meetings lasted ninety days. We had a water baptismal service every Sunday for seven weeks. When the meetings were over, we had baptized almost every kind of relative we had.

We moved into the city of DeLeon, Texas, for a meeting which lasted six weeks. There are a number of ministers over the country who were saved in those meetings.

A few years ago we were invited back to that county for the fortieth anniversary of the fire falling. What memories were shared! I shudder to think how near I came to not going that first time. I learned early to obey the Lord, and my life has been richer because of it.

20

GOD'S PRESENCE
FILLED THE TABERNACLE

Thomas Paino, Sr.

My mother brought my brothers and me to the United States from Ireland when I was seven years old. How I have appreciated the privilege of being in America with its freedom to worship God!

I was in officers' training in Camp Lee, Virginia, when the flu epidemic of 1917-18 began. Men all around me were dying, and I made a vow to God that I would serve Him if my life was spared.

Although I was spared, my wife contracted tuberculosis. When the war was over, I took her to Tupper Lake, New York, hoping to receive help. It was there that God began to change the whole course of our lives.

My wife was wonderfully converted in a street meeting conducted by a Methodist minister who had been filled with the Holy Spirit. The minister had a book, *Signs and Wonders*, written by Mrs. M.B. Woodworth-Etter describing her forty-five years of ministry to that time. After reading the book we went to Indianapolis, Indiana, to have Sister Etter pray for my wife's healing.

Although I believe in prayer and God's ability to heal, I would not attend Sister Etter's meetings because I was a

Catholic and a third-degree member of the Knights of Columbus. (In those days good Catholics did not attend other churches.)

I was a wretched sinner but I wanted to do right. One night a sister invited me to a meeting, and I couldn't refuse. I said to myself that I had committed all manner of sin anyway, so one more would not matter.

At the meeting I heard singing, shouting , messages in tongues and interpretation. The people testified how they were saved, filled with the Spirit, and healed.

Oh, I thank God for the presence of His glory that filled the tabernacle that night. God put a hunger in my heart to seek Him. No one had to ask me to go to the altar. I wanted what God had given these people. That night was only the beginning of my seeking God.

For eight weeks I prayed, confessed, and repented of my sins. The more I prayed and sought the Lord, the hungrier I became for the things of God. Oh, the joy, love, and peace that flooded my soul! On December 26, 1919, God baptized me with the Holy Ghost and fire.

After God called me to preach the gospel, we had the privilege of being co-workers with Sister Etter in some of her great revivals just before she went to her reward.

In 1922 we started on our own. Holding meetings in rented halls or tents, we saw churches started in almost every place we preached. God confirmed His Word with signs and wonders in every meeting.

In 1933 we were called back to the church in Indianapolis where I had come to know the Lord. During the years at West Side Gospel Tabernacle we have seen many churches started from the home church. Nearly one hundred of our young people are preaching the gospel.

Much credit is due to my faithful wife who has not only been a good mother to our children but a wonderful co-pastor and preacher as well.

21

CALLED TO PREACH

Aaron A. Wilson

In 1914 a Hebrew-Christian evangelist, Pauline Kern, came from Chicago to the little town of Farrenburg, Missouri, where we lived. A "Holiness" couple, Brother and Sister Simpson, invited her into their home for services. The attendance was such they moved into the Dunkard Church and continued, God honoring His Word with a revival that stirred the whole countryside. Many souls were redeemed from sin in that area where a revival had not come for years.

My sister and her husband were saved. After much prayer and persuasion my wife and I went to see and hear. I am glad we did, for the gospel of Christ moved our hearts and we were gloriously saved. My father also was saved—my mother was already a Christian. My grandfather and two uncles being Baptist preachers, we cast our lot with the Baptists and organized a church which was much blessed of God.

About two years later we heard of a strange religion where folk spoke with other tongues. They had come to the town of Parma, Missouri, where my two Baptist preacher uncles lived. One of them attended the services and heard them preach the full gospel—salvation from sin, baptism in the Holy Spirit, divine healing, and the soon coming of the Lord. He was convinced of the truth and was wonderfully baptized in the Holy Spirit.

The other uncle was bitterly opposed and called my father to come and try to rescue his brother from this "Pentecostal heresy." However, when Dad attended the meetings he felt like the officers who went to arrest the Lord Jesus and who said, "Never man spake like this Man." He listened, believed, and arranged for one of the preachers, W.C. Anderson, and his wife to come to our place. A great number of people were saved and filled with the Spirit.

This time of searching the Word and of searching hearts, confessing our sins and humbling ourselves, brought God into action. The people, as in Elijah's day, saw His mighty works and said, "The Lord, he is God." My life was completely changed. I entered into a relationship with God never known apart from the baptism of the Holy Ghost (John 14:20).

I had felt the call to preach from a child, but when filled with the Spirit *such* a burden for lost souls came upon me! My precious wife was wonderfully filled with the Holy Spirit and miraculously, instantly healed. But we passed through many trying experiences before I would yield to the call to preach. We gave up two children, ages two and four, just fourteen hours apart. That brought me to deep, serious thinking. Two of my older friends, F.L. Doyle and John T. Wilson, talked with me and prayed much with me, encouraging me to obey God.

I first preached for my pastor, S.B. Drew, in Parma, Missouri, where we were members. Next I preached in Jones schoolhouse, Risco, and Canalou, Missouri. I received my license to preach in Advance, Missouri, at a camp meeting. E.N. Bell was the Bible teacher and John T.

Wilson and Arlie Ellsworth were the evangelists.

I was called to pastor a church in Puxico, Missouri. On my way there I had to spend several hours at Bloomfield, Missouri, before the train arrived. I had little money, so I fasted at noon and read Evans' book *How to Prepare Sermons*. After five years as pastor in Puxico I was elected district superintendent. I resigned that office after five years and went to Kansas City, Missouri, where I pastored for thirty-one years.

Today our Captain, the Lord of Hosts, is still leading the way. One day, perhaps very soon, He will take us to be with Him, not for a few days of blessing, but to be together forever.

22

NEWSPAPER REPORTS KANSAS REVIVAL

It is doubtful whether in recent years anything has occurred that has awakened the interest, excited the comment or mystified the people of this region (Galena, Kansas) as have the religious meetings being held here by Rev. C.F. Parham, familiarly termed, "Divine Healer."

Over three months have elapsed since this man came to Galena and during the time he has healed over a thousand people and converted over eight hundred. When Rev. Parham first began to attract attention he was holding services in a large tent and soon the streets in that vicinity were crowded nightly with people who were anxious to see and hear the wonderful man who was healing the sick, the maimed and the blind, without money and without price. When it was found that the tent was utterly inadequate to accommodate the crowd which assembled, a large double storeroom that would shelter two thousand people was procured, a platform was built at one end, stoves were set up, rough pine boards were installed to be used as seats. Here the past six weeks Parham has preached to a crowded house and the interest shows no sign of abatement. In this rude temple, cures that are looked upon almost in the light of miracles have been performed. During the services there have been as many as fifty people at the altar at one time seeking to be restored in soul and body. Here people who have not walked for years without the aid of crutches have risen from the altar with their limbs so straightened that they were enabled to lay aside their crutches, to the astonishment of the audience.

These cures, they claim, are affected solely through prayer and faith. Nothing else is done, though Rev. Parham often lays his hands upon the afflicted one while the devotions are going on, with the result that some say it is due to his own magnetism that so much is accomplished.

Parham and his followers do not advocate Christian Science or Spiritualism, but their belief condensed is that God is able to overcome all, cure diseases of both body and soul, and will do so if they live a consecrated Christian life and depend on Him for all.

"The Healer" makes no charges and takes no credit upon himself, saying that he is only teaching the people the "true way." He takes no collections during the meetings, but, notwithstanding, has had the needs of himself and family well provided for by donations from a grateful public.

Mr. Parham is a light, spare man extremely delicate looking, and, in fact, he has said that he was an invalid and badly crippled until he was healed through prayer. His face is pale and earnest looking, while masses of brown hair cover his remarkably shaped head. Mr. Parham is the possessor of such a wonderful personality that some have accused him of hypnotizing his followers.

Others go as far as to term him a fanatic, but one and all regardless of sect or prejudices, agree that he has brought about conditions that were never before witnessed in this section. Evening after evening the large room is packed with people, many of whom "have gone to scoff but remained to pray."

Here the man of prominence and position clasps hands with the uneducated son of toil or oft times of those who have had a prison record back of them. Here women who have formerly lived for society and gaiety, kneel beside some fallen sister and endeavor to point her heavenward. Here the "followers" receive what they term "the Pentecost" and are enabled to speak in foreign tongues, languages which they are, when free from this power, utterly unfamiliar with.

One evening recently (New Year's Eve meeting) over four hundred remained at the meeting the entire night singing, praying and speaking in different languages. Not until daylight did they disperse and a strange sight they presented, wending their way homeward in the gray light of the morning.

On another occasion hundreds congregated on the banks of Spring River during one of the coldest days in winter and witnessed Mr. Parham immerse almost one hundred converts in its icy waters, not one of whom, however, contracted even a cold.

But of all the wonderful things which have transpired in connection with these meetings nothing has attracted the attention of the public as has the "healings" which have not been confined to an ignorant, uneducated class of people. On the contrary, some of the most conservative, intelligent persons, not only here, but within a radius of over a hundred miles, have visited "the healer" with wonderful results.

The list of those who benefited by Rev. Parham's visit to this section is indeed a large one and has done much to regard the man with almost superstitious awe, but when one meets him in his everyday life he is so quiet, so unostentatious, so sympathetic, that he invariably wins confidence. His wife is in every sense of the word a home woman and heartily in sympathy with her husband's work, although on account of the three little ones is necessarily not able to take a very active part in it. However, her sister, Miss Thistlewaite, is a close attendant at the meetings and an earnest worker. The Parham home, or "stopping place," as they call it, is always full of visitors, some of whom have come many miles to consult "The Healer," others are objects of charity, whom the people are befriending. In the last two weeks branches of the Parham meetings have sprung up in almost a dozen of the different mining camps of this district all of which are attracting large crowds and it is difficult to enter a company where the wonderful results of these meetings are not the chief topic of conversation.

23

WHEN THE "HOLY ROLLERS" CAME

E. L. Tanner

My wife and I were full of curiosity when we were told, "The Holy Rollers are coming!" We wondered why these strange religious people would expect folk to go to revival services through the deep mud of country roads such as we had in the little community of Summerfield, Louisiana.

The weather was cold and rainy when the strangers arrived—seven adults and one child—in January 1913. My father and two uncles, trustees of the Methodist Church, gave them permission to hold services there. None of them claimed to be a preacher, but all sang, testified, and explained the Scriptures.

Word got out that it was not a safe place for women and children, so only a few men and boys went at first. Finally one night a doctor broke the ice by bringing his wife and children, and others followed. The church was filled every night.

The first young man to respond to the altar call was picked up by two other men and carried from the altar.

A few nights later, to my great surprise, the first one at the altar was my wife! We had been married almost a year, and I knew her to be a quiet, timid person. Remembering the stories of how these folk supposedly would "hypnotize" people, I moved closer to see that nothing should happen to her.

As I sat watching her pray, she suddenly threw up her hands and began praising the Lord for salvation. Soon she began to sing in an unknown tongue as the Holy Spirit rested upon her. I was convinced that this was the work of God, although I was not saved until several months later.

In the summer of 1913, we attended a camp meeting at Malvern, Arkansas. There we met E. N. Bell whose paper, *World and Witness*, had been an inspiration to us. When I went to pay him for a Bible I had ordered by mail, Brother Bell said to me, "I have no accounts against my brethren. Pay me what you remember the price to be."

I marveled at this fellowship into which we had come.

Evangelist Mary Woodworth-Etter came for the last few nights of this camp meeting. As she prayed, both a deaf-mute child and lady dying with tuberculosis were instantly healed.

One night we were thrilled to hear the heavenly choir join the earthly voices in a song. Sister Etter had asked the choir to stand and sing, "Holy, Holy, Holy," and to yield to the Spirit for she believed the Lord was going to visit the meeting in a special way. As they sang, my wife and I, as well as the whole congregation, heard a separate and distinct choir of voices blending perfectly with those of the singers before us. The sound of music and voices came in from the front, then swelled to fill the entire large tent above our heads, and finally lifted to fade away in the distance. It was truly heavenly and not of this earth.

At the beginning of our Pentecostal experience we made a complete consecration to God. Our ministry began in homes; then we held meetings in brush arbors, schoolhouses, open air, and finally tents. We had one tent in which to live and another for services. During the winters I would work, and in the summer we ministered wherever we found an open door in northern Louisiana. There are now churches established in almost all the places we preached during those early years.

In May 1924 we came to West Monroe, Louisiana, and the Lord helped us establish a church which we served for some thirty years. God performed many miracles in this city. One was the healing of my wife in 1952.

When she became very ill, the doctor X-rayed and found she had cancer too far advanced for surgical help. The whole congregation went to its knees in prayer, and the Lord heard and answered by healing her completely. X-rays later showed no trace of the cancer. We do give God all the glory.

24

AFRICAN LANGUAGES SPOKEN IN THE SPIRIT

Fred Burke

I was a country boy when God laid His hand upon me. At the age of fifteen in 1916, I became a student in Beulah Heights Missionary Training School. After some weeks during which I sought God earnestly, He came to me late one night as I waited before Him. My whole being was flooded with His power, glory, and unspeakable joy. There flowed forth from my lips volumes of praise to God in another tongue. I seemed literally to have entered the presence of God.

After forty-five years of active service on the South African mission field, may I be permitted to "analyze" the experience of that night? Has it stood the test of time? Has it helped me on the field?

In its first impact it changed me from a timid boy who feared to stand up in a service—even to give a short testimony—to one who could stand confidently before congregations, knowing it was not I who spoke but God's Spirit speaking through me as I yielded to Him.

For me the baptism was the incoming of a *Person*, not a momentary ecstatic experience. He had come to direct my life. As I followed Him, doors opened; needs were miraculously supplied; difficult circumstances were changed. He had come to lead me. "As many as are led by the Spirit of God, they are the sons of God."

The baptism signaled the incoming of a *Revealer*. He is the Spirit of wisdom and revelation. "He shall take of mine, and shall show it unto you." Just before this mighty infilling of the Holy Spirit, He led me through the judgment hall to the Cross. Standing before the Cross I was melted and broken before God. It was not a vision, but the sufferings of Christ were made so real it was as if I had been there. And then upon my broken spirit God poured out His Spirit to fill me with Himself.

It was the incoming of a *Helper*. He is the Comforter, the "One-alongside-to-help." Soon after arriving in South Africa I began to study the Zulu language. I found this language with its "clicks" difficult, but one evening at prayers I felt prompted to pray out in Zulu. Within a very short time I was testifying and then preaching in Zulu. Africans said to me, "Why is it that when you are preaching, you speak so fluently; yet in ordinary conversation you find it hard to speak our language?" It was that I had a divine Helper.

Later, at the invitation of Ralph M. Riggs, my wife and I went to Vendaland and began to labor among a more primitive people. The Spirit again became my Helper in a special measure. Finding it difficult to speak through an interpreter who did not understand me, I dispensed with his help and in a very short time was preaching in the language of the Venda people.

In Nyasaland (Malawi) while still pioneering, I again felt led to dispense with the interpreter. To his great surprise I began speaking directly to the people in their language. (All this does not mean that I did not have to spend time in language study, but it does mean that the Holy Spirit's anointing enabled me to use what I had studied without hesitation while preaching.) Mission work is so much easier with the Helper.

The baptism for me was the incoming of a *Teacher*. "He shall teach you all things." As I was riding muleback in Vendaland, the words of a hymn began to come to me in the Venda language. I wrote it down, and this continued until I had written a book of Venda hymns, some translations, some composed.

Years later, working again among Zulu-speaking Africans, the same thing occurred; and another book was printed. The Spirit began to urge me to write Bible study books in African languages. As I obeyed, a number of courses were written and are being used in many parts of Africa to train ministers by correspondence.

Soon after I arrived in Zululand, tropical sores began to spread over my limbs. Then, while I was alone in my hut, the Spirit of God came upon me in wonderful power, and He said, "I have healed you. Remove the bandages!" The sores dried up almost immediately.

I was very ill with fever when one night the Spirit came mightily upon me, rebuking the fever in another tongue, and I was delivered. Again and again He has quickened my body.

Recently as I meditated there came to my soul an upsurge of glory, and the Scripture was illuminated to me, "In whom also, after that ye believed, ye were sealed with that Holy Spirit of promise, which is the earnest of our inheritance." Not only is the Holy Spirit our Helper, Guide, Teacher; He is in Himself, in the joy and glory He imparts, a *foretaste of heavenly joys*. So with heaven in our souls, we are journeying to the heaven above, in preparation for which we have been washed in the blood of Christ.

Fifty years in Pentecost have only made these truths more real, and the Spirit Himself more precious.

25

FATHER AND SON HEALED TOGETHER

David H. McDowell

When I arrived in Waynesboro, Pennsylvania, in January 1908 to become pastor of a Christian and Missionary Alliance mission, I found a small company of sincere believers. Some had come in contact with Pentecost, and many were hungry for God.

We supplemented our Sunday and Tuesday services in the rented mission hall with cottage prayer meetings. These were well attended, and a number received the baptism in the Spirit. Among those attending the prayer meetings was a couple who had a child about four years old who had never walked. He was carried to the cottage services and needed constant care.

In almost every service we would pray definitely for him, holding him under the arms and encouraging him to use his wobbly little legs. But as soon as we let go of his arms, he would flop right down to the floor. After many such efforts I began to commit the child to the Lord and wait for more light and help in his case. But we never gave up hope that the Lord would heal him in His own time.

The father of the child had the worst case of bronchial

asthma I had ever seen. His breathing could be heard by everyone in the service and it was quite disturbing at times.

One Sunday evening after the service was dismissed he spoke to me about his condition. He said he was going to take the Lord as his Healer and asked me to anoint him and pray with him. I called some of the elders, and we prayed earnestly.

When he arose from his knees, he walked over to our large "bung-hole" stove; it was a cold night, and a good fire was burning in the stove. He opened the door and emptied out all his medicines which he carried with him. He said, "When I get home, I'm cleaning out my medicine cabinet also, for it is loaded."

On the way home I said to my wife, "We are in for a genuine test of faith if we have never had one before!"

All went well until we were leaving our house for the Tuesday evening service. One of the ladies of the church came rushing up all out of breath. When she could speak, she said, "Brother McDowell, you'll have to get over to Brother Pittinger's. He's in a terrible condition. He has been sitting by the window in the parlor and bending over until he almost touches the floor, then pulling up with all his might to breathe up and down constantly. If he doesn't get help, I'm sure he'll die."

I sent Mrs. McDowell on to open the church service and started off running to Second Street where the Pittingers lived. It was a starlit night, and the heavens were clear. As I rushed down a slight grade, I suddenly stopped, looked up and cried out to God. Then on I ran, feet scarcely touching the ground.

As I rounded the corner at Second Street I glanced across the street. The shade was drawn at the Pittinger's window, but I could see his shadow—down then up, down then up. I didn't stop to rap on the door but broke into the hallway and right into the room. I caught him as he was on the coming-up stroke. I put my hands on his head and began a powerful rebuke in tongues as the Holy Spirit moved me.

Immediately he jumped to his feet and started running around the room, hands high and praising God, breathing to the bottom of his lungs. I stood there watching and thanking and worshiping God.

As I had pushed the door open into the room, it had stopped against the end of the couch. I was startled as I heard a noise and a little shout as the boy who had never walked bounced down off the couch and started running after his daddy. His hands were in the air, and he was singing childishly, "Oh, glory, hallelujah, I am on my way to heaven, shouting glory. . . ." It was one of our cottage prayer meeting songs.

This child who had never stood, much less walked, was healed in a split second and able to walk and run. God is faithful!

Some twenty years later I had an assignment that took me to Waynesboro. As I walked down the street, a young man said, "Why, hello there, Brother McDowell."

I said, "You have the advantage of me. . . ."

"Don't you know me?" he asked. "I'm the boy who was healed the night you prayed for my father when he was about dead with asthma."

To say I was amazed puts it mildly. This fine young man was perfectly well, a walking testimony to the healing power of God.

26

WORSHIPING IN THE SPIRIT

Leland R. Keyes

My introduction to Pentecost occurred in a mission in an eastern city. (In the early days we did not call our places of meeting churches; they were Pentecostal missions.)

In this particular mission where I was to be both saved and filled with the Spirit, there was one custom which attracted my attention and drew me toward the Lord.

A Spirit-filled lady, known to be a godly and devoted believer, was used of God in a very simple manner. She would go to the organ (just an old-fashioned pump organ) before the service began, and play the old familiar songs that had become Pentecostal favorites. She played them under anointing of the Spirit and would sometimes begin to sing, also under an anointing.

As the people gathered for the service they would join in this beautiful, deeply devoted singing. God came down. His presence was wonderfully real. A spiritual atmosphere was created that prepared the way for the service to follow. Somehow there was no problem of talking, whispering, or other preservice noise and confusion. Such would have been alien to the spiritual atmosphere that was engendered by this simple informal singing and playing before the service began.

Nothing had to be "worked up" or "brought down" by the efforts of the leaders. There was no need to try to produce a spirit of worship; it was already there. A Spirit-baptized body of believers, loving the Lord with all their hearts, singing and making melody in their hearts to the Lord, expressing their joy in songs and hymns and spiritual songs in the public assembly, prepared the way for what was called "a Holy Ghost meeting."

The gifts of the Spirit were manifested, and the Word of God was proclaimed in the power of the Spirit. The result was that the altars were filled with those who were hungry for God.

It was in such an atmosphere that I came to know the Lord and to receive the fullness of the Spirit.

One of the members of this Pentecostal mission, a godly "mother in Israel," was given a vision. In her vision she saw the building filled with the saints of God, sitting in their usual places, worshiping God. Then, as though the ceilings were lifted off the building, she saw demon spirits around the rim of this rectangular building with their fiery darts which they were constantly aiming toward the believers seated in the worship service. But between these demonic powers and the people of God there appeared a thick, blood-red cloud. Each time a fiery dart was shot toward the believers, it was unable to penetrate this thick cloud. Instead, the fiery dart would be deflected by this protective covering of a blood-red cloud. The saints of God suffered no harm.

One cannot help but be reminded that in the exodus from Egypt the Lord provided a cloud which stood between the people of God and their enemies; in fact, the cloud struck terror into the hearts of those who would have destroyed them.

Thank God for the blood of the Lord Jesus Christ that covers those who put their trust in Him. It is their protection from all the fiery darts of the enemy. By day and by night, God's blood-washed people shall dwell securely.

27

THE RIGHTEOUS SUFFER

William Emanuel

I remember an April evening in 1907 when my mother and I attended a revival meeting being held in a schoolhouse in Wauchula, Florida. This was the first Pentecostal meeting held in South Florida, if not in the entire state. F.M. Britton, the evangelist, had received the Holy Spirit baptism a few months before under the ministry of G.B. Cashwell, a Holiness preacher from Dunn, North Carolina. Cashwell had received the Pentecostal experience in 1906 at the Azusa Street Mission in Los Angeles.

I still remember the profound impression made upon my heart by the first words I ever heard spoken in an unknown tongue. I was deeply convicted of my sins and sought the Lord for salvation. After I was saved, I continued to wait upon the Lord for the infilling of the Holy Spirit but did not receive the experience until some years later.

Souls were being saved and filled with the Spirit in the revival when the authorities stepped in and closed the schoolhouse doors to the evangelist. However, a small Seventh-Day Adventist church was made available, and the meetings continued day and night—sometimes all night.

Many seekers were "slain" under the power of the Spirit. Some would lie prostrate for hours, then burst forth in a heavenly language. Others were entranced by a vision of the coming of Jesus.

And I remember a tragic incident that occurred at the close of the revival. I relate it now as a fragment—albeit a sad one—of Pentecostal history of that early day. A former preacher who had drifted away from the Lord, attended the revival services almost from the beginning. He sought the Lord earnestly, but seemed unable to pray through to victory. I think I have never heard a more impassioned prayer than the one he prayed on the last Sunday morning of the revival. The words seemed to pour out in an anguished torrent as though coming from a soul in an agony of remorse. It was in all probability the last prayer he ever prayed. In some way the devil had deluded the poor man into believing that he had sinned away his day of grace—that the gift of the Holy Spirit was not for him, and that his condition was hopeless.

That afternoon, the last day of the revival, at a spot some two hundred yards from the banks of Peace River where a baptismal service was in progress, this unfortunate victim of Satan's deception stabbed himself and died within a few minutes.

This regrettable tragedy brought bitter persecution to the Pentecostal believers. The townsfolk assumed, mistakenly, that the man had been a convert of the revival and that the "new" religion had led directly to his self-destruction. The antagonism was so strong that the work came to a virtual standstill. However, home prayer meetings were held from time to time, and the fire of God still burned in the hearts of His people.

The day came when a Pentecostal church was built in the community, so the cause of Christ triumphed over the scheme of Satan to discredit the Pentecostal testimony in the first town in which it was proclaimed in that area. Today there are thriving Pentecostal churches in the town. They stand as monuments to the faith, prayers, and sacrificial efforts of a little band of believers who remained faithful to God and their Pentecostal experience in the face of fierce opposition.

28

MIRACLES IN SOUTH AFRICA

John G. Lake

One Sunday afternoon a tall Englishman walked into my church in Johannesburg, South Africa. He had a top of red hair that made him as conspicuous as a lion. He walked up the aisle and took a seat quite near the front. My old preaching partner was endeavoring to explain the mighty power of the living Christ as best he could, and this man sat listening. Presently he arose, saying, "Sir, if the things you are talking about are all right, I am your candidate."

He added, "I used to be a Christian, but I came to Africa and lived the usual African life and the result is that for three years I have been unable to do anything and my physicians say I am incurable. Tell me what to do."

My old partner asked, "John, what shall we do?" I replied, "Call him up; we shall pray for him right now." We stepped off the platform, put our hands on William T. Dugan, and instantly—as a flash of lightning blasting a tree or rock—the power of God went through the man's being, and the Lord Jesus Christ made him well.

A few days afterward he came to my house in the middle of the day and said, "Lake, I want you to show me how to get a clean heart." I took the Word of God and went through it with him to show him the mighty, cleansing, sanctifying power of the living God in a man's heart. Before he left he knelt by a chair and consecrated his life to God.

Three months passed. One day he called and said, "I have a call from God." I knew it was. There was no mistaking it. The wonder of it was in his soul. He went down into the country where a great epidemic of fever raged. Some weeks afterward I began to receive word that people were being healed. Hundreds of them! Thousands of them! One day I concluded I would go down and join in the same work a couple of hundred miles from where he was. Somehow the news traveled to him where I was, and he came there.

The next afternoon we called at the home of a man who said his wife was sick with diabetes. We prayed for the wife and several other persons who were present. Then a man stepped out into the kitchen and asked, "Would you pray for a woman like this?" When I looked at her I saw she had club feet. The right foot was on an angle of 45 degrees and the left at right angles.

Dugan replied, "Yes. Pray for anybody." He said to her, "Sit down," and taking the club foot in his hands he said, "In the name of Jesus Christ become natural." And I want to tell you that man is in the glory presence of God today and I am going to stand there with him some day. Before I had a chance to take a second breath that foot commenced to move, and the next instant that foot was straight!

Then he took up the other foot saying, "In the name of Jesus become natural." Beloved, it was not the voice of the man, nor the confidence of his soul, but the mighty divine life of Jesus Christ that flashed through him and melted that foot into softness and caused it instantly to become normal by the power of God.

Another man, Von Shield, was a book agent in South

Africa. He began to attend our meetings, and one day when I was not present he came forward out of the audience and knelt at the altar and sought God for a conscious knowledge of salvation. And bless God, he received it.

Some days after that when I was present and teaching at an afternoon service, he raised up in his seat and said, "Lake, do you suppose that if God gave me the baptism in the Holy Spirit it would satisfy the burning yearning that is in my soul for God?" I replied, "My son, I don't know that it would, but I think it would go a long piece on the way."

So without more ado he came forward, knelt and looking up, said to me, "Lay your hands on my head and pray." And as I did the Spirit of God descended in an unusual manner. He was baptized in the Holy Spirit very wonderfully indeed and became a transformed man. From that hour that man was a living personification of the power of God. All my life I have never found one through whom such majestic intense flashes of power would come at intervals as through that soul.

Presently he disappeared. His father came to me saying, "I am troubled about Harry. He took a Bible and went off into the mountains almost three weeks ago. I am afraid he is going insane." I answered, "Brother, do not worry yourself. One of these days he will come down in the power and glory of God." I knew what was in that fellow's heart.

One day he returned under such an anointing of the Spirit as I have never before witnessed on any life. Not long after that he came to me and said, "Brother Lake, did you know this was in the Bible?" And he proceeded to read to me that familiar verse in the sixteenth chapter of Mark: "These signs shall follow them that believe; in my name shall they cast out devils." Looking up into my face with great earnestness, he said, "My! I wish I knew somebody that had a devil!"

I believed God had planned that situation, for I was

reminded that in my mail a couple of days before had come a request for an insane son. The mother wrote, "As far as I can tell, my son has a devil." She requested that we come and pray that the devil might be cast out.

Von Shield said, "Why this is only a couple or three blocks from where I live. I am going to find this fellow, and then I am coming back for you."

I said to myself, "Here is a newborn soul, whose vision enters into the real realm of God-power." I realized that my own spirit had not touched the degree of faith that was in that soul, and I said to myself, "I do not want to say a word or do a thing that will discourage that soul in the least."

Presently he came back and said, "Brother Lake, come on." We went and found a boy who had been mad from his birth; he was like a wild animal. He would not wear clothes and would smash himself or anybody else with anything that was given him. He couldn't even have a dish from which to eat. But in the center of the enclosure where he was they had a large stone hallowed out and they would put his food in that and let him eat it just like an animal.

We tried to catch him, but he was wild as a lion. He would jump right over my head. Finally his father said, "You will not catch him out there." I had been somewhat of an athlete in my youth, and I said to Von Shield, "You get on one side and if he comes to your side you will take care of him, and if he comes to my side I will take care of him."

This all sounds strange, I know, but I'll never forget that afternoon as long as I live. As I looked across to that young man I could see the lightning flash of faith, and I knew that if he got his hands on that man the devil would come out.

Presently he landed on my side of the bed, and in an instant Von Shield sprang over the bed, laid his hands on his head and commanded the devil to come out. In two minutes that man was absolutely transformed, and he became a sane man, the first moment of sanity that he ever knew.

29

AN UNUSUAL EXPERIENCE IN THE UPPER ROOM MISSION

Ruth Carter

How can one describe the movings of the Holy Spirit in the human life? Or the glory of His presence in a service?

In 1906 my father (Elmer Fisher), who had been a Baptist pastor, received the baptism in the Holy Spirit. The following year he opened a Pentecostal work which became known as the Upper Room Mission (Los Angeles). His motto was, "Exalt Jesus Christ; honor the Holy Ghost." There was revival for many years in the Mission, with two services a day five days a week. The morning Bible studies were conducted by George Studd, a gifted, Spirit-filled Bible teacher, brother of the famous missionary C.T. Studd.

The Upper Room Mission was in a large hall on Mercantile Place (which later became an arcade) between Spring and Broadway, and Fifth and Sixth, in the heart of Los Angeles.

One Sunday afternoon in the fall of 1913, God moved in an unusual way in the service. I was only a girl, seated beside my mother on the front seat. As the blessing of the Lord began to fall like dew during the song service, the people began to worship in the Spirit. There were several hundred present, and all seemed oblivious to everyone else as they worshiped. The sacred Presence was so real that one after another the people stood to their feet, hands upraised, eyes closed, lost in worship.

The chorus of praise began to unite them. Even those who ordinarily were hardly able to carry a tune sang like opera singers. Then it blended into such harmony, without a discordant note. It was what we called the "heavenly choir." As the cadences of this supernatural song rose and fell, the beauty of it was beyond description.

I had always loved the Lord, but I had not yet been filled with the Spirit. Now my heart too was full of worship, but I was very timid. If I stood to praise the Lord, someone might see me. However, as far as I could see, all had their eyes closed. I reasoned that I too could stand and praise Him whom my soul loved, then sit down before anyone else did, and no one would notice me. So I stood.

I cannot explain what happened. I only know that I was utterly unconscious of my surroundings as I joined in that heavenly chorus, lost in adoration as my soul reached out to Him.

When I opened my eyes everyone was seated, and I sat down hastily. Later I learned I had been standing alone for some time, worshiping in the language of heaven. The people, after the heavenly song had ceased, had been seated, and waited quietly in the presence of One who had filled a little girl with His Holy Spirit. Something else was also accomplished in that meeting where program was set aside while the Spirit moved, though it was several years later that I heard the story.

A man who had been healed of blindness under my father's ministry held a meeting in the church my husband (the late Wesley Steelberg) served as pastor. He told of having been in the service that afternoon in 1913. He was sitting toward the back of the hall when a stranger came in and sat beside him. Later he learned that the man was a music teacher—and an agnostic. He had been walking along the street below the open windows of the hall when he heard singing. He stopped to listen—such harmony, such blending of chords he had never heard. Whatever could it be, he wondered. Finding the stairway he came up to this large auditorium, seating himself beside our friend. He sat entranced until the music ceased. Then a conversation somthing like this followed:

"What is this?"

"This is a gospel meeting."

"But who taught the people to sing like that?"

"No one taught them. It is God."

"But how did they learn such harmony?"

"They did not learn it; it was given by the Holy Spirit."

The stranger could not understand it, but sitting in that hall with God's presence so real, he felt there must be a God. The singing he had heard had some supernatural quality. It would take God to do that.

Under deep conviction he yielded his life to God. It is possible that no preaching could have convinced him of his need as the Holy Spirit did that afternoon through a congregation yielded to Him.

30

MRS. ETTER
ANSWERS CRITICS

Mary B. Woodworth-Etter

The ministers of the city (Springfield, Illinois) tried to crush me and the work in our meeting during January and February, 1889. They brought history, doctor books and the devil's works to prove that the power of God had been taken from the church. When they got their ammunition ready, they chose Dr. B. of the Christian church, the great theologian and champion debater, to fire off the cannon.

Dr. B. announced that he was going to prove me a fraud and drive me out of the city on the strength of it. He drew a large crowd and took up a special collection. Many of the citizens took notes and brought them to me. They said it was the weakest thing they ever heard, and they were disgusted. The night I was attacked, our hall was packed—the people thinking that I would denounce him. After the congregation had gathered, God gave me a text which I had never used before. "Come and hear, all ye that fear God, and I will declare what he hath done for my soul" (Psalm 66:16).

I gave a sketch of my experience from my birth to the present. People were weeping in all parts of the building. I do not think there was one there who did not believe God had called me to the work, and that He was with me in mighty power, working wonderfully in the midst of the people. I did not intend to reply to Dr. B's arguments. I had said that I would meet anyone on the Bible. He had gone outside of it for nearly all his proof. The citizens were very anxious for me to reply. Finally I announced that I would meet him on Sunday night. The hall was crowded and hundreds were turned away.

It was an undertaking to meet this giant. He boasted of his college courses, of his education, of his wisdom, of his popularity, and made it appear that I was a poor, ignorant, blinded crank. I am a crank for Christ, and the devil cannot turn me. My trust was in God. I set my face like flint, for God was with me, knowing that no weapon raised against me should prosper, and every tongue raised to condemn me I should confound.

When I arose to talk the congregation was as still as death. I held the paper in my hand that contained Dr. B's arguments, and referred to one after another and proved them to be false. He said that I had failed in every scriptural test, and that I was a fraud. I said the best proof of our being called of God to preach was the fact that souls were saved. I asked all who had been converted in these meetings to stand. Over two hundred stood.

I asked all who had their bodies healed by the power of God to stand. About fifty stood. The people said that before I had taken the Bible in my hand, I had cut his head off with his own sword. I met all his arguments on the Bible and did not go outside it. I proved him to be wrong on every point. Glory to God for the victory! With all his boasted wisdom he spoke. But God chose a weak woman to confound and condemn and show to the world that it was useless to fight against Him or the Holy Spirit power.

Not one minister stood by me in Springfield. All united in

opposing and trying to crush me. Notwithstanding, all this power of darkness that was arrayed against me, the interest in the meetings increased daily. Requests came from leading citizens from all over the city to stay. Many of the brightest talent in the city inquired about the way of salvation. Old gray-haired fathers thanked us, with tears streaming down their cheeks, for leading their children to Christ; wives whose husbands were saved from drunkard's graves thanked me for coming to Springfield.

Glory to God for the victory!

31

THE FAITH OF
JOHN ALEXANDER DOWIE

Lilian B. Yeomans, M.D.

It has been my privilege to know personally some men and women who have had outstanding results in the healing ministry. One of them was Dr. John Alexander Dowie.

I met Dr. Dowie in about 1900. He introduced himself and talked about the meaning of his name: John, "by the grace of God"; Alexander, "a helper of men." As for the Doctor, it had been bestowed upon him by grateful people who were healed in answer to his prayers.

While I could never fully follow Dr. Dowie in all of his teachings, I could not doubt the truth of his statement that God had given him gifts of healing. The Holy Spirit answered it to my soul, and he was approved of God by miracles and wonders and signs which God did by him and which the man in the street could neither deny nor resist.

I once asked one of the very best dentists in Chicago what he thought of Dr. Dowie. He did not know that I was acquainted with him. He replied, "Well, it is impossible to deny the genuineness of his healings; how he does them I cannot explain, but he does them without the shadow of a doubt. I myself know a young lady whose leg was lengthened three inches and who now stands straight. You can see her any Sunday in Dr. Dowie's choir."

When Dr. Dowie began his work in Chicago, in 1893, I think it was, he set up a wooden hut at the World's Fair and rang a dinner bell to get the people to the meetings. He had some wonderful healings, including the healing of Ethel Post, a little girl of about thirteen whose mouth was so full of a bloody, spongy cancer that she could not close it day or night.

The surgeons would not touch the cancer for fear she would bleed to death, for the blood vessels in it were so infiltrated with cancer cells that they would not hold ligatures. As Dr. Dowie drove across Lincoln Park to pray with her, the Lord gave him the verse that He is God to kill and make alive (2 Kings 5:7), and he prayed, "O Lord, kill the cancer and heal the child."

The malignant growth withered away and fell out of the girl's mouth and throat, and she was completely and permanently healed. When I alluded to her case in a meeting quite recently, a lady stood and said Miss Post is alive and well and actively engaged in some branch of commercial art. She used to sell her photographs, "Before and After the Lord's Healing Touch," for the benefit of the Lord's work.

I visited at Dr. Dowie's Divine Healing Home in 1898. It was then on Michigan Boulevard, Chicago, and was a most luxurious hotel fitted in modern style. But it had something I had never seen in any other hotel: a staff of helpers filled with faith in the Word of God. Their faces shone, and any one of them—from the furnace man to the elevator boy—was ready to preach you a sermon at a moment's notice if you dared to doubt that Jesus Christ is the same yesterday, today, and forever.

Dr. Dowie's devotion to the Word of God was beautiful.

He would read it to sick folks for hours on end—sometimes not even stopping for dinner. As he read they would visibly lift up their heads like flowers after a gracious shower. I have known him to put dinner back when it was served . . . because he said we needed the Word so much more. He simply brought you right up against the Word, "I am the Lord that healeth thee," and expected you to believe it.

Dr. Dowie had invincible, God-given faith in the Word of God as being the same today as it ever was and ever will be. . . . If there was anything in his personal life or his teaching that was not in accordance with God's Word, you are not called upon to follow it. But I exhort you to imitate his faith in God's Word.

32

THE MINISTRY OF A FORMER MODERNIST PASTOR

Dr. Charles S. Price

I want to take you by the hand and lead you down the corridors of the years, letting you look into some of the scenes of my ministry as an evangelist.*

My first meeting was at Ashland, Oregon. The Ministerial Union invited me and rented a building that seated more than the population of the town. It was soon packed to the doors. All the churches of the city were closed for the meetings and, having told the ministers that I was going to preach the whole truth, I proceeded to do so.

The power fell. Hundreds were saved and hundreds were healed. The first person that I prayed with for bodily healing fell under the power of God. I was afraid. I prayed for the second one and the same thing happened. I trembled in the presence of the Lord; but both of them, rising to their feet and proclaiming they were healed, gave me courage and I

---

*By his own admission, Dr. Charles S. Price was a modernist. But he was converted and received the baptism in the Holy Spirit in a meeting conducted by Aimee Semple McPherson in 1922.

went on praying. After that scores and scores would be prostrated under the power at one time. An adjacent building was rented so great became the crowds, and the meeting continued longer than its advertised time.

From Ashland I went to Albany (Oregon). One of my very closest friends, Rev. Thomas J. McCrossan, pastor of the United Presbyterian Church, had been down to the Ashland meeting and returned to Albany with reports of what the Lord had done. Dr. McCrossan became convinced that the whole movement was of God. . . . The ministers engaged the Albany Armory and from the very first service it was packed to the doors. Quite often the crowd would stay in the building from ten o'clock in the morning until the time for the night meeting. We had to beg people, who were Christians, to stay away in order to allow the unsaved to find room. Practically the entire high school class gave their hearts to Jesus; and it has been reported that it was impossible to hold a public dance in town for one year after the campaign because there were not unconverted girls enough with whom to dance. It was a mighty revival. I want to quote from Dr. McCrossan's own book at this point so that you might get some understanding of what happened in that meeting.

"Dr. Price came to Albany with five churches behind him. At the very first service, Sunday afternoon, scores came to Christ. At each service . . . the altars were crowded with seekers. Many nights we had to vacate two, three and even four rows of chairs on the wide platform to accommodate the great overflow of seekers. Some of us ministers had been through campaigns with Moody, Torrey, Gipsy Smith, Wilbur Chapman, Biederwolf, F.B. Smith, French Oliver, Billy Sunday and other really great evangelists; but it was the unanimous opinion that we had never before found men and women under such tremendous conviction of sin as in this campaign. Very frequently from fifteen to twenty-five persons over sixty-five years of age were at the altar weeping their way to God. Here they found such a depth of conviction, the deepest by far they had ever experienced, that they knew for a surety this was the work of the Holy Spirit.

"At the first healing service in Albany I was fully convinced that God did heal the sick through prayer. The second person to be prayed for had a very large goiter. Dr. Price touched her forehead with oil, and then placing his hand upon her head offered a simple prayer that the Lord would then and there give her faith to accept. She is well today. We ministers felt withered hands and arms, time and again, which were cold and useless. Within an hour after being prayed for, those same hands and arms would be as warm as our own. Is it any wonder that we believe in divine healing?

"The last Saturday night was the greatest soul-winning service of the campaign. We ministers were all assisting Dr. Price, who was anointing some four hundred sick persons seated on the main floor, and we followed to pray for those anointed. While thus engaged, God's Spirit took possession of the meeting. Without any invitation being given, sinners began to flock to the altar; old people seventy years of age and scores of young people. Young converts came forward bringing their weeping companions. Soon the altar and the whole stage were crowded with seekers, and everywhere in the house people began to fall under the strange power of God. We preachers had read of such scenes in Finney's meetings, but we had never expected such experiences ourselves. . . . As a result of our meetings hundreds were saved. One church received over 100 members, another 75, another 60, and another 50, but most of the converts were outside the city.

"At Roseburg, Eugene, Victoria, and Vancouver, B.C.,

this same wonderful soul-winning power was evident. At one afternoon service in Roseburg, we counted thirty-five persons from sixty-five to eighty years of age kneeling at the altar seeking Christ. The oldest ministers in all these cities have admitted to me that in all their experience they have never seen God's soul-winning power so displayed. In both the Victoria and Vancouver campaigns there were days when from seven hundred to one thousand persons came to the altar, all under the same tremendous conviction of sin."

Dr. Price Continues the Story

I have quoted from the pen of Dr. McCrossan because I know my readers will appreciate the opinion of one so well known in the religious world. How wonderful was my Lord to take a self-willed, proud preacher like I had been and fill him with His Spirit! We give Him the glory for it all.

From Albany we went to the First Methodist Church of Eugene. Once again the power fell. We were forced to move to the spacious armory and that too became crowded to the doors. Out of that meeting there was built Lighthouse Temple which was one of the most spacious auditoriums in the entire full gospel movement at that time. During the Eugene campaign miracles of healing occurred that shook the entire countryside, and denominational preachers were filled with the Holy Ghost.*

It is with a feeling of deep humiliation and eternal gratitude to God that I recount these events. There is a sense in which I dislike putting them down in this record, for fear that some should think that the ego is asserting itself too much. God forbid. I am only a sinner saved by grace; and it is for the glory of the Lord alone that I tell of the marvelous things that the Lord has done. I am reciting these events to show you what God can do with a man who will lay himself on the altar and seek until he is filled with the Holy Spirit. If

there was any power in the meetings, it was the power of
God. It was not mine. As a matter of fact, I rejoiced on the
days when God took the meetings out of my hands and
manifested Himself in such marvelous and glorious ways
that all the people wondered!

---

*One of the miracles in the Eugene campaign was the
healing of the editor's father, thirty-seven-year-old
Harry E. Warner, who was suffering with cancer. He
lived to be ninety-one.

33

A REVIVAL AMONG CHILDREN IN POLAND

Oskar Jeske

During the summer of 1916 when I was fourteen, I was saved as a result of my mother's prayers and a revival in our area of Poland. That was the most wonderful day in my life.

In the fall when our school opened for classes, God began a work among the children. My grandfather, who was our schoolteacher, greatly respected the Bible and religion but was not a believer. He was hardly ready for what was to happen that Friday afternoon as he began to teach the class a Bible lesson on Abraham and the sacrifice of Isaac. I remember the day as if it were yesterday.

After the portion of Scripture was read, Grandfather gave a few words of introduction. The children in the room interrupted him with questions as he compared the sacrifice of Isaac and the sacrifice of Christ.

Suddenly the seventy-one children in the class were stirred by some invisible power and began to weep. Grandfather, who was annoyed at the display, shouted at us and ordered silence. But his shouting was to no avail and the sobbing grew louder. Grandfather picked up a yardstick and beat it so violently on the table that it broke into several pieces. He again commanded silence, but to no avail. Getting up from his desk, he paced up and down the classroom several times. Finally, he motioned for me to leave my seat. Then, nervously, he left the room.

I arose and went to the teacher's desk. I took my New Testament from my pocket, read a few verses, and spoke about them as well as a fourteen-year-old is able. After I had spoken for a few minutes, the children all knelt as if by command and began to pray loudly. It was so loud that one could not hear oneself speak, so I tried to restore order and finally succeeded to some extent. None of the children had remained mere onlookers; all were under the influence of the Holy Spirit.

When it was possible for me to speak again—I still had to shout to make myself heard—I admonished the children, telling them not to shout so loudly but to come to Christ in faith and accept His salvation. It was not by weeping and shouting, I told them, that we have salvation and the forgiveness of our sins but by faith alone. I spoke for three or four minutes and then the children began praying a mixture of requests and thanksgiving. I went from desk to desk, praying with some, encouraging others, still in an extremely loud voice.

The result of this Bible lesson? Of the seventy-one children present that day, fifty-one were converted.

The lesson had begun at one-thirty in the afternoon, and I found it difficult to send the children home at seven o'clock that evening. Our experience that afternoon was so great that even Grandfather stood shaking his head not knowing what to say.

While the children knelt praising God, I heard several of them say things that I could not understand. They spoke a language which was unknown to me, and yet it seemed to be a complete language. Shivers ran through me as if I had been in contact with an electric current. It seemed rather uncanny but at the same time it was like a balm from heaven.

I knew nothing at that time of the baptism in the Holy Spirit and speaking in tongues. Yet I knew immediately that God had given us a miracle brought about by His Holy Spirit. Not until 1926 when I found Christians who spoke in other tongues did I realize that the children on that afternoon had been baptized by the Spirit and had indeed spoken in other tongues.

A similar event occurred in the following week, although not on the same scale. Even Grandfather did not leave the classroom this time but watched while I prayed individually with the children. At four o'clock he suddenly interrupted us and told the children to go straight home. Because it was not cold we went to a nearby woods and continued our prayer meeting until nightfall.

Following our prayer meeting at school, a new wave of revival came to the village, for the children went home with joy and tears, asking parents and friends for forgiveness. Many had stolen fruit from neighbors' gardens; some had done worse. All confessed and explained why they were confessing. Parents, children, and neighbors could scarcely believe what was happening.

At this time God particularly revealed Himself among the children, giving them visions. One afternoon about thirty of us had gathered together shortly before sunset. Suddenly we saw splendid angelic hosts such as Jacob must have seen on his flight to Laban. We were deeply affected and trembled as we gazed at the throng of heavenly hosts.

When the angels vanished, one of the children remarked, "Just like the time when Jesus was born."

The church meetings now began to be even better attended, resulting in a different need. Because the school children now also came to the meetings, there was no room large enough to hold everyone. People could truly say when they heard the children praising God, "Out of the mouths of babes and sucklings thou hast perfected praise" (Matt. 21:16).

34

GOD IS FAITHFUL

G.W. *Hardcastle*

In the early days of the Pentecostal Movement anyone who obeyed the call to the ministry was simply on his own to trust God for his needs. There was little or no financial support for either evangelist or pastor. Consequently, a deep consecration and a willingness to suffer for the cause of Christ were indispensable qualifications for the Pentecostal ministry.

My wife and I would go to places where none sympathized with us or believed our message. One such occasion we were driving an old car with a canvas top so worn that it was torn completely off in a windstorm. Having a white wagon canvas with us, we wrapped and tied it over the bows of the top. Thus we drove into a small town in southwestern Colorado one Sunday afternoon in our patched-up car. A Methodist Church permitted us to hold a revival since they had no pastor. The town was small, but people from various denominations came to the services and the crowds were large.

We took the message of Pentecost to a small city where it had never been preached before. After many unsuccessful efforts to secure land to set up our tent we found a place with the help of the county judge and began our meeting. When we made our first altar call we saw many men and women come seeking salvation and the baptism in the Holy Spirit.

This brought the wrath of some, and a mob was formed for the purpose of whipping me and running me out of town. The message of holiness was the message most hated by the ungodly in those days, and probably this is still true today.

On our way to a youth convention we passed through a very attractive little city in an area we had not previously visited. God seemed to impress me that we should conduct a revival there. The district superintendent would not encourage us to do this, since previous efforts there had been unsuccessful. However, in a miraculous way God proved it to be His will for us to go there.

In the natural, our situation was discouraging. We had no one to underwrite our expenses, and no money of our own, and four small children to care for. The city boycotted us, but after two weeks (including four days of fasting) God broke through.

Although we had not been accepted at first, and were twice ordered by the city attorney to close the meetings, God moved upon that city until without a word of advertising we had the tent filled and overflowing onto the five lots around it. In six weeks we set a church in order with thirty-seven adult charter members including some of the leading people of the city.

Yes, I remember the hardships of those pioneer days, but I remember too the joy of trusting God who never failed. There were times when with small children to feed we had no food in the house. At such times we would not drop a hint to an earthly friend, but just send up a reminder in faith to our Heavenly Father, and a bountiful supply would come in.

God has met many desperate needs for us. When

blindness seemed certain, I was instantly healed. After twenty-one days of lingering pneumonia and typhoid, my wife was instantly healed through prayer. Then there was the miraculous healing of our son, G.W. Hardcastle, Jr., who is now pastor of Evangel Temple in Kansas City, Missouri.

David's memory of his victory over the lion and the bear gave him courage to meet Goliath. And so the memory of God's grace in the time of small needs gave us courage to trust Him in more trying circumstances. This life is fuller and has more assurance as we meet the present with the memories of past victories. I believe we are made strong for whatever lies ahead only as we suffer victoriously the adversities of the present. It is said of Christ, "Though he were a son, yet learned he obedience by the things which he suffered."

35

REVIVAL IN CANADA

Lilian B. Yeomans, M.D.

My sister and I were getting ready to move to California from our home in Canada when some folks in a rural part of Alberta invited us to hold meetings in their area. We accepted the invitation and started the long drive to the place.

Since the car was in poor shape and the roads were bad, it seemed that we had to pray the old car along every foot of the way. When we finally arrived we began immediately to teach and preach in schoolhouses and homes and visit the sick. We also prayed with believers who were seeking for the baptism in the Spirit. We had the joy of seeing God move in a blessed way.

After a few days of blessing there, we decided it was time to return home and complete arrangements for our move to California. So we bade them all a loving farewell and asked them to have the famous car ready for an early departure the next morning.

Quite late that night, a man called to see us, bringing his wife and family. He was an unbeliever, and I noticed that one of his little boys had a marked squint in one eye. I told the parents that it was not God's will that the little thing should be so deformed and afflicted and that we would pray for him if they wished. They agreed so we laid hands on the child in the name of Jesus, and then they went home. I cannot remember that I noticed any change in the eye directly after we prayed, but as we were very busy seeing people who came to say goodbye, it may have escaped our notice.

Early the next morning before we had finished breakfast the man returned and reported that the child was so improved that they were all amazed and recognized God's hand in the healing. He asked us to stay a while longer and promised to come and bring his family to the meetings . . . which meant something as he lived a long distance from the place we were holding the meetings.

We decided that the happening was a token from the Lord that He still had work for us to do there. We announced that we would continue the meetings, inviting all who were really seeking the baptism in the Holy Spirit, but *no others*, to attend a tarry meeting in the upper story of our host's barn that very evening. It was a wonderful barn, the finest one in the whole district.

And I certainly shall never forget that meeting; it was in some respects the most wonderful meeting I ever attended.

As I was on my way to the meeting, I saw a man with a most unhappy expression on his face . . . casting longing glances . . . toward the huge gray barn. I called to him and asked him if he wanted to come to the meeting.

"Yes," he said, "I want to come but I am too bad a man. I am known all over this district as a bad man. My wife is at the meeting; she is a godly woman, but I have led her an awful life. I am a bad man."

"Well," I said, "you are the kind the meeting is for, for the worse you are the more you need Jesus. We are going to seek Him there tonight as Saviour, Healer, Baptizer, and All in

All. Come along."

So the "bad man" (we'll call him John) accompanied me to the meeting. Maybe the people were shocked to see him come, but that was not as shocking as what happened later.

The people knew almost nothing about the baptism; and since they were from various churches and societies, I explained the way of full salvation in the simplest manner possible, including the baptism in the Holy Spirit according to Acts 2:4. I told them to look to the Lamb of God and praise Him for all He had provided for them. And they began. Everybody expected John's wife to receive the baptism first because she was considered the best person in the district.

I can see those people now if I close my eyes. It was a beautiful loft, a real "upper room." The floor was covered with new mown hay and the whole place lighted by lanterns hung around the walls. The faces of the seekers looked so earnest in the flickering lantern light. There was a spirit of love and harmony.

John knelt on the outside of the ring where the shadows were deep as the lantern light hardly penetrated to that distance. I wondered how he was getting along and intended to go over and pray with him; but before we had been on our knees many minutes, the power fell and a sister—not John's wife—received the baptism. As she was kneeling next to me she fell over on me and I could not get away.

When John's wife actually heard this sister praising God in other tongues, she seemed to grow desperate in her longing and began with all her might to call upon God for the baptism.

I was encouraging her when suddenly as a flash of lightning the power of God struck John where he was kneeling, bolt him upright at the edge of the group, and then felled him to the floor with a crash so mighty that it seemed as though it must pull the building down. And he lay there under the power which moved and manipulated every part of his body with such force and lightning-like rapidity that the people thought he was having an awful attack of convulsions. Indeed it was with great difficulty that I calmed their fears. At last the Spirit began to speak through him, first in English, describing the vision he was having of Calvary. Would to God that every sinner in the world could have heard him! It would have melted a heart of stone. And after that he spoke with awesome power and majesty in a new tongue.

His wife was so dumbfounded when she heard him that she said to me: "He's got the baptism before me, and he was *so* bad. Perhaps I need to be saved from my goodness more than he needed to be saved from his badness."

And I said, "Perhaps you do. Just repent of everything and cast yourself on Jesus."

Just then, to the amazement of all, John raised himself to his knees and made his way over to us. Then he preached the most wonderful sermon on Calvary I ever heard. It was thrilling. He seemed to see Jesus and to be able through the power of the Spirit to make us see him too.

As he kept pointing his wife to Calvary, the power of the Spirit touched another sister and she danced around the loft lighter than a feather . . . and singing meanwhile in Gaelic. Later her language changed to high German, which I could understand a little. And she was unable to speak in English for two days. When people would speak to her in English, she would answer in German. And the amazing thing about the entire experience was that she had never learned German!

These were days of heaven on earth. The power of the Holy Spirit fell on many others, saving and baptizing in the Spirit.

A heaven-sent revival came to that place as a result of the healing of that small boy! Praise God!

36

HEAVEN ON EARTH

Ralph M. Riggs

My first contact with Pentecost was in Hattiesburg, Mississippi, in 1909, when I was fourteen years old. There I attended a short-term Bible school where Hugh Caldwalder, Joe Roselli, William McCafferty, D.C.O. Opperman, and Howard Goss were ministering.

From my home in Meridian, Mississippi, I later traveled to Fort Worth, Texas, to attend a Pentecostal camp meeting. There I was baptized in water by A.P. Collins, who later became the second General Chairman of the Assemblies of God.

In June 1913 a camp meeting was held in Meridian. Bennett Lawrence from Thayer, Missouri, was the camp speaker. He later invited me to go back to Missouri with him. We stopped en route at Malvern, Arkansas, and there I met E.N. Bell, the convener and first Chairman of the Assemblies of God.

It was while I worked with Brother Lawrence as song leader at Thayer that W.T. Gaston came to hold a tent revival. Here I was baptized in the Holy Spirit on August 29, 1913. I can still remember singing, "Joys are flowing like a river, since the Comforter has come." In the church at Thayer I also received my call to preach while simply singing, "I'll say what you want me to say, dear Lord."

I preached my first sermon that summer on the text, "Have faith in God." My partner in this, my first revival, was John Sappington. In the meantime we had moved to Memphis, Tennessee, and the next spring I went with my pastor, L.P. Adams, to Hot Springs, Arkansas, to attend the organizational meeting of the Assemblies of God. I remember well the messages preached by M.M. Pinson and John G. Lake (just returned from South Africa) at those historic meetings in Hot Springs in April 1914.

There were not many Bible schools in the land in those days but a copy of *Trust*, a periodical from Rochester, New York, fell into my hands. On the flyleaf of that little paper was an announcement concerning the Rochester Bible Training School which was conducted in connection with "Elim," a faith home operated by Mrs. E.V. Baker and her sisters, Hattie and Susan Duncan. I left my job (clerking in a grocery store in Memphis) to go "way up north" to Rochester in September with the only straw hat in town!

For two happy years I sat under the deep spiritual teaching of the Duncan sisters and of John Wright Follette. They left an indelible impression on my life. Just at graduation time a delegate from Syracuse, New York, came to the school to find a young man to pastor a little group of saints. I was recommended and off I went to Syracuse. We worshiped in a lodge hall on the third floor of a downtown business building, but eventually we bought an abandoned old-fashioned movie house and named it "Grace Tabernacle."

In my Bible reading one morning, I started to read the forty-ninth chapter of Isaiah. Immediately I became aware that the Lord was speaking to me from His Word. The fourth and fifth verses described what I had been trying to do for three years at Syracuse. The next verse was His direction for me. "I will also give thee for a light to the Gentiles, that thou mayest be my salvation unto the end of the earth." This was my call to the mission field.

I had always been interested in missionary work in Africa, and now I had His command to go. Without money or support I started out. Like most pioneer missionaries these days I was led step by step. Every need was supplied just as it arose. I had heard of a Pentecostal work in South Africa sponsored by Bethel Pentecostal Assembly of Newark, New Jersey. I wrote volunteering as a missionary. I was accepted and in the spring of 1919 I went overseas.

Those priceless early days of the Pentecostal Movement hold many precious memories. They were indeed the "good old days" of which Carl Brumback has written so interestingly in his fascinating book, *Suddenly from Heaven* (now published as *Like a River*, Gospel Publishing House). I bear witness to the truthfulness of his account of the Heavenly Choir which so impressed Professor Wittich at Elim, and the accompaniment of an angel's voice with a duet of boys on two occasions, for I was there and heard. Those were indeed days of heaven on earth.

But there were also occasions when imposters came, speaking in tongues. (In those days speaking in tongues seemed to be sufficient evidence that they were God's men!) The imposters worked their frauds on unsuspecting people and escaped just one step ahead of the sheriff! Perhaps the Pentecostal Movement has been sobered somewhat from those "good old days" but it has overcome many weaknesses too.

One thing more should be said. There was a great evangelistic zeal in the early days and a reckless penetration into unconverted lands and areas, homes and hearts all around us. We must retain this "first love." The fire must never go out. May God help us to win the lost in our neighborhoods and everywhere. May every heart be set ablaze with the Pentecostal flame and may it burn forever.

37

WHEN THE FIRE FELL

Dexter E. Collins

In 1922 there was a remarkable outpouring of the Holy Spirit in the small town of Wellston, Oklahoma.

This was our first pastorate. The church had been without a pastor for some time previous to our coming, and the people were discouraged. After several months of effort to increase interest, we felt led to call a special prayer meeting to begin on Monday morning at nine and to continue without dismissing throughout the week. At the end of the first week we announced the meeting would continue another week.

Only three came at first. During the second week, interest increased. Members of the church began to confess to each other and to ask forgiveness. By the end of the week a revival had begun.

Prayer meetings were held each day the third week, and evangelistic meetings conducted in the evenings. Many were saved, and eleven received the baptism with the Holy Spirit.

Among the converts during that week was a very hardened sinner whose Christian wife had been praying for him for more than a year. He was not saved in a church service, however. The meeting that night was already in progress when he came in and interrupted to tell what had happened.

He testified that he was convicted of his sins while cultivating corn late that evening. His conviction was so great, he said, that he tied the horses to a fence post, went to a nearby grove, and prayed through to a wonderful experience of salvation!

(All this took place after his wife had gone to church. She was hearing it along with the rest of us for the first time.)

He told how his wife had prayed for him to be saved, and how he had resented and cursed her for praying for him, but now he thanked God for answering her prayers. With tears of joy this man told how he had marked the place in the grove where the Lord had gloriously saved him, by driving a wooden stake into the ground.

Then, as we used to say, "the fire fell," and great conviction come upon all who heard his testimony. This revival continued for over a year.

The following summer a big brush arbor was built near the town, and another advance prayer meeting was held before the beginning of eight nights of evangelistic meetings. Brother Jacob Miller of Arkansas was the evangelist.

During those eight memorable nights, 120 people received the baptism with the Holy Spirit, and many were saved.

One night, two men who had never been in a Pentecostal revival before drove forty miles in a farm wagon to be in the meeting. They had heard how people were receiving the baptism with the Holy Spirit, and they were very excited about it.

They arrived a few minutes before the service was to start, and they asked what they should do to receive the baptism with the Holy Spirit. I instructed them to get as close to the altar as they could, and told them that when the invitation was given they should get to the altar as soon as possible. Afterward I could not get to them for the crowd, but I could see that each of them received a mighty baptism of the Spirit within a few minutes' time after they began praying.

As a result of those meetings in 1922 and 1923, more than three hundred were saved, and some two hundred received the baptism with the Holy Spirit. Nineteen entered the ministry either as missionaries, ministers, or wives of ministers.

I still believe there is no substitute for intercessory prayer for a revival. This is the divine pattern, and it has never failed to produce results.

38

FAITH IS THE VICTORY

J.P. Kolenda

In the fall of 1927 I accepted the pastorate of a newly formed church in Flint, Michigan. The enthusiastic congregation of about forty people had just purchased a nice brick church building, seating about two hundred fifty. Although this was commodious for our congregation, I could not rid myself of a feeling that the snug little church was inadequate for the challenge of Flint, a growing industrial city. When I mentioned this in one of our board meetings, the response was, "Young man, let's fill this church first and then talk about a larger building."

The following summer Evangelist C.E. Roberts conducted a campaign in a wooden tabernacle seating fifteen hundred people. When I learned the tabernacle was to be sold later, I asked the evangelist if he would give me the first chance to buy it. He agreed to do so.

Meetings continued nightly in the tabernacle for eleven weeks. Many churches cooperated, and God blessed. The tabernacle was filled almost every night and crowded on Sundays. Toward the end of the campaign I met with my church board and proposed the purchase of the tabernacle.

They pointed out that the people had attended services for many weeks and were tired. Also, it was November and would soon be too cold to have services in the tabernacle. Their arguments were logical and reasonable; still I pleaded with them to buy the tabernacle.

Impatiently one of them said, "All right, pastor; if you feel it is God's will, you buy it. But you know that according to the treasurer's report there is no money on hand, and we are behind on our church payments."

This would probably have ended the matter had not one of the board members come to my rescue. He said, "Brethren, you see that this is a matter of conviction with our pastor. It is true we have no money and Brother Roberts needs cash for the tabernacle. Perhaps we can borrow the amount."

After some discussion the willing board member finally said, "Very well, I will try to borrow the money on my property."

Thankful and happy I left the meeting and could hardly wait for a favorable reply to the man's application for a loan.

About ten days later I went to his home to inquire about it, only to find there were some problems. Some personal difficulty had taken place since our meeting, and he rather abruptly reported that the bank had denied the loan. "Furthermore," he said, "I am resigning as a member of the board."

I stood speechless, my last hope for the tabernacle fading, when my eyes fell on a little yellow promise-box card on his table. Absentmindedly I picked it up and put it in my pocket.

Finally I said to him, "Very well, my brother. We will talk about this matter some other time."

I walked home in a daze and locked myself in my room. I was determined not to leave until I had heard from God. As I examined my heart, I cried, "Lord, is it my vain ambition or is it Thy plan and will that is being frustrated?"

In the agony of my soul I put my hand in my pocket and felt the little card. When I looked at it, I read, "Have faith in God" (Mark 11:32). Billows of joy swept over my soul. I laughed and could not stop laughing. It was the laughter of faith, not in men but in God.

An hour later I left my room with a holy confidence. I went to see the evangelist and told him we would buy the tabernacle.

"Good," he said. "Did you get the money?"

"No," I replied. "We will buy it without any down payment and will pay $100 a month until paid for."

"What makes you think I can sell it on these terms?" he asked.

"I know you can," I replied confidently.

He looked at me a little while, then said, "I don't know why, but I will take you up on your offer."

We had to move the tabernacle to another lot, and since the new lot was next to Flint River, we called it "Riverside Tabernacle." All winter long we kept on with special meetings. Many times when the temperature was below zero outside, more than a thousand people were enjoying God's blessing inside. Hundreds of souls were saved; many were filled with the Holy Spirit. We never could have gone back to our little brick church.

Good men of God followed us as pastors in Flint. The work developed; a large and beautiful sanctuary and educational buildings were erected near the center of the city. Riverside Tabernacle continues to be a source of blessing to many, proving that it is worthwhile to "have faith in God."

39

THE REVIVAL AMONG THE GIRLS OF MUKTI, INDIA

Minnie F. Abrams and Albert Norton

In January 1905, Pandita Ramabai spoke to the girls of Mukti concerning the need of a revival, and called for volunteers to meet with her daily to pray for it.* Seventy volunteered, and from time to time others joined until at the beginning of the revival there were 550 meeting twice daily. In June, Ramabai asked for volunteers to give up their secular studies and to go out into the villages round about to preach the gospel. Thirty young women volunteered. We met daily to pray for an enduement of power.

On June 29, at 3:30 A.M., the Spirit was poured out upon one of these volunteers. The young woman sleeping next to her awoke when this occurred and seeing a fire enveloping her, ran across the dormitory, brought a pail of water and was about to dash it upon her when she discovered that this girl was not on fire. In less than an hour nearly all of the young women in the compound gathered around, weeping,

---

* Pandita Ramabai was a well-educated Indian widow who was converted during the latter part of the nineteenth century. She started a home for widows at Mukti.

praying, and confessing their sins to God. The newly Spirit-baptized girl sat in the midst of them, telling what God had done for her and exhorting them to repentance.

The next evening while Pandita Ramabai was expounding John 8, the Holy Spirit descended and all the girls began to pray aloud. All in the room were weeping and praying, some kneeling, some sitting, and some standing, many with hands outstretched to God. God was dealing with them and they could listen to no one else.

From that time the two daily meetings of the praying band became great assemblies and the Bible School was turned into an inquiry room. Girls were stricken down under the power of conviction of sin. Regular Bible lessons were suspended, and the Holy Spirit Himself gave to the leaders such messages as were needed by the seeking ones. After strong repentance, confession, and assurance of salvation, many came back in a day or two saying, "We are saved, our sins are forgiven. Now we want the baptism of fire."

One Sunday the text spoken from was, "He shall baptize you with the Holy Ghost, and with fire" (Matt. 3:11). The Holy Spirit evidently taught the girls through this passage and the one in Acts 2:1-4, as well as through the experience of the first baptized girl, to expect an actual experience of fire; and God met them in their expectation. They cried out at the burning that came into and upon them. Some fell as they saw a great light. While the fire of God burned, the members of the body of sin, pride, love of the world, selfishness, uncleanness, etc., passed before them. There was much suffering for sin under view of the self-life. . . . Finally complete assurance and joy took the place of repentance. Some who had been shaking violently under the power of conviction, now sang, praised, and danced with joy. Some had visions, others had dreams. The Word of God confirmed all this. The Holy Ghost had been poured out according to the Scriptures. Such seeking could not have been endured except that it was done in the power of the Spirit. They neither ate nor slept until victory was won. Then the joy was so great that for two or three days after receiving the baptism in the Holy Spirit they did not care for food.

A Missionary's Eye-witness Account
Albert Norton *

We began to hear of Christian believers in different places and countries receiving the gift of speaking in a new tongue which they had never known before. One day I visited the Mukti Mission. Miss Abrams asked me if I should like to go into a room where about twenty girls were praying. After entering, I knelt with closed eyes by a table on one side. Presently I heard someone praying near me very distinctly in English. Among the petitions were "O Lord, open the mouth; O Lord, open the mouth; O Lord, open the heart; O Lord, open the heart; O Lord, open the eyes! O Lord, open the eyes! Oh, the blood of Jesus! Oh, the blood of Jesus! Oh, give complete victory! Oh, such a blessing! Oh, such glory."

I was struck with astonishment as I knew that there was no one in the room who could speak English, beside Miss Abrams. I opened my eyes and within three feet of me on her knees with closed eyes and raised hands was a woman whom I had baptized at Kedgaon in 1899. My wife and I have known her since as a devoted Christian worker. Her mother tongue was Marathi, and she could speak a little Hindustani. But she was unable to speak or understand English. . . . But when I heard her speak English idiomatically, distinctly and fluently, I was impressed as I should have been had I seen

---

*A missionary stationed at Dhond. The revival later spread to Norton's school for boys and sixty-five were baptized in the Holy Spirit.

one whom I knew to be dead, raised to life.

Again I was at Mukti . . . when some twenty-four persons had received the gift of tongues. Quite a number had received the ability to speak in English, a language before unknown to them. Just why God enabled these women and girls to speak in English instead of Tamil, Bengali, Tugulu, or some other language of India and unknown to them, I cannot say. But I have an idea that it is in mercy to us poor missionaries from Europe and America who as a class seem to be doubting Thomases in regard to the gifts and workings of the Spirit, and are not receiving the power of the Holy Spirit as we ought.

40

I'LL LOOK FOR HIM
IN HEAVEN

David H. McDowell

I met a certain man only once—on May 5, 1908, but I believe our meeting was divinely ordained. We were on a train bound for New York City.

Miss Marie Burgess, who later became Mrs. Robert Brown, was opening a mission at 454 W. 42nd Street, in New York City. She had invited me to be the special speaker, an honor extended to me annually since that time, on the anniversary of that humble beginning of Glad Tidings Tabernacle.

I was young and inexperienced, pastor of a small mission at Waynesboro, Pennsylvania. I had been filled with the Spirit the year before, but it was with a sense of helplessness that I looked forward to this new experience in public ministry as I boarded the train at Harrisburg.

My main problem was how to find enough sermon material for a two-week stretch. To me that was a big order. My thoughts turned to the Jewish question, for the massacres of Jews in Russia had been much in the news. While thinking along this line I noticed a man on the opposite side of the car and a few seats forward reading a foreign-language newspaper. The Lord spoke to me as He did to Philip in the desert (Acts 8:26-29): "Go over and join yourself to this man."

I hesitated, and the word came again: "Go over and join yourself to this man."

I still questioned and then I felt the presence of the Lord lifting from me. It was not imagination, believe me! So I said, "Lord, I'll go."

I walked down the aisle to where the man sat. He lowered his paper and looked up at me questioningly. "May I speak to you for a moment?" I asked. He moved over politely, and I sat down.

"I see you are reading a Jewish newspaper," I began.

"This is not a Jewish paper."

I saw at once he resented being identified as a Jew. I was embarrassed and wondered if I had been mistaken. Then I asked him, "Could you give me any information on the Jewish situation in Russia? I am deeply interested in the Jewish question."

"No, I don't know anything about the Jews in Russia. I am a businessman in Philadelphia."

At this moment I felt the Spirit of God come upon me, and suddenly it was as though I were another person. Turning toward the man I raised my arms and found myself speaking in another tongue. This continued for several minutes.

In shocked surprise the man asked, "Why didn't you tell me you were a Hebrew?"

"I am not a Hebrew."

"You are not a Hebrew? Where did you get this language? You speak to me in purest Hebrew. You tell me more about my people than I know. We don't speak that language anymore; we speak Yiddish. You go to college?"

"No."

"You study Hebrew?"

"No."

"Tell me. What kind of man are you? You don't go to college; you don't study Hebrew; and you speak to me in the finest Hebrew. I am puzzled."

It was then time to open my New Testament. Calling him Abraham, I said, "If you will listen to me now, I will give you the answer. I am of Scottish parents. I have been converted and have accepted your Messiah as my Saviour, and He has baptized me in the Holy Spirit." Then I began to read to him the first and second chapters of the Acts. Believe me, you never saw such a surprised man. He was speechless.

We were pulling into Broad Street Station in Philadelphia, and he reached for his handbag. I picked up the bag and went out to the platform with him. Tears flowed down his cheeks as he said, "I wish I were going with you."

Still calling him Abraham, I said, "Buy a New Testament and seek your Messiah. He will fill you with His Spirit as He has filled me and many others, and we will meet in heaven. Good-bye now."

The whole experience took me by such surprise that I did not think to get his real name or to give him mine. But I believe I shall meet this Jewish man again—in heaven.

EPILOGUE

Most of the events recorded in this book happened during the early twentieth century. This was the period that saw the birth of the modern Pentecostal Movement—the counterpart of today's Charismatic Movement.

These Pentecostal pioneers blazed a trail in those early days that has blessed a world. They were human—just as we are. They made mistakes—just as we do. Yet they dared to trust God when the Pentecostal message was despised, persecuted, and ridiculed by church leaders and unbelievers alike. These are people listed in God's Hall of Fame.

But what about today? Does God still save hardened sinners like the man Lillian Yeomans describes in "Revival in Canada"? Does God still heal the sick as he healed the twentieth-century Lazarus under the ministry of Smith Wigglesworth? Does God still perform miracles like the multiplying of the bread as told by Oskar Jeske? Are people receiving the baptism in the Holy Spirit today?

Yes, these things are happening today and even on a wider scale. The Pentecostal Movement that you read about in this book has grown up and is thriving in the free countries of the world. Then who can count the number of believers in the Charismatic Movement that touches every Christian organization?

It is good to look back at what God accomplished through these Pentecostal pioneers. But let's not rest there. There are still hardened sinners who need deliverance and peace, there are still people who hurt and need healing, there are still millions of people who need to hear about the Lord Jesus Christ, there is still a need for the miraculous. This generation needs to be touched by the same fire.

Ralph Riggs summed it up in his chapter "Heaven on Earth." "There was a great evangelistic zeal in the early days and a reckless penetration into unconverted lands and areas, homes, and hearts all around us. We must retain this 'first love.' The fire must never go out. May God help us to win the lost in our neighborhoods and everywhere. May every heart be set ablaze with the Pentecostal flame and may it burn forever."

The fire must not go out.

Wayne E. Warner

ACKNOWLEDGMENTS

Grateful acknowledgment is given authors and publishers of material used in this book. Without their cooperation and permission this book would not have been possible.

"The Healing of a Twentieth Century Lazarus," from *Ever Increasing Faith*, pp. 28-33, by Smith Wigglesworth, Gospel Publishing House, Springfield, Missouri, 1924.

The following stories were reprinted from two series of articles that appeared in the *Pentecostal Evangel*, © 1964 and 1966 by the Assemblies of God, Springfield, Missouri: "Preserved Though Poisoned," "My First Earnest Prayer," "I Heard the Angels Sing," "God Healed My Father," "A Vision for the Lost," "I Found the Best in Life," "The Ministry of 'Brother Tom,' " "My Personal Experience at the Azusa Mission," "Personal Experiences of Divine Healing," "It Took a Miracle," "I'm Glad I Obeyed the Lord," "God's Presence Filled the Tabernacle," "Called to Preach," "When the 'Holy Rollers' Came," "African Language Spoken in the Spirit," "Father and Son Healed Together," "Worshiping in the Spirit," "The Righteous Suffer," "An Unusual Experience in the Upper Room Mission," "God Is

Faithful," "Heaven on Earth," "When the Fire Fell," "Faith Is the Victory," and "I'll Look for Him in Heaven."

"God's Moving at Azusa Mission," adapted from tract "A Sparkling Fountain for the Whole Earth," by Rachael A. Sizelove, n.d.

"Living by Faith in Egypt," quoted in *Lillian Trasher, The Nile Mother*, pp. 84-88, by Lester F. Sumrall, Gospel Publishing House, Springfield, Missouri, 1951.

"Raymond T. Richey, God's Pinch Hitter," quoted in *They Saw It Happen*: by Gordon Lindsay, Christ for the Nations, Dallas, Texas, 1972. Originally published in *What Hath God Wrought!* by Eloise May Richey.

"The Multiplying of the Bread" and "A Revival Among Children in Poland" from *Revival or Revolution*, pp. 24-26, 27-30, by Oskar Jeske, Full Gospel Publishing House, Toronto, 1970.

"Mrs. Etter Answers Critics" and "When God Visits St. Louis" from *Marvels and Miracles*, pp. 61-62, 63-71, by Mary B. Woodworth-Etter, published by author, Indianapolis, Indiana, 1922.

"An Outstanding Healing in Toronto" from *Grandmother Flower's Story*, p. 4, by Alice Reynolds Flower, n.d.

"Memoirs of the Azusa Revival" from *What Really Happened at Azusa Street?* by Frank Bartleman, published by the author in 1925.

"Newspaper Reports Kansas Revival" was published in the Cincinnati *Enquirer*, January 27, 1904, quoted in *Suddenly . . . From Heaven*, by Carl Brumback, Gospel Publishing House, Springfield, Missouri, 1961.

"Miracles in South Africa," quoted in *John G. Lake, Apostle to Africa*, by Gordon Lindsay, Christ for the Nations, Dallas, Texas, 1972.

"The Faith of John Alexander Dowie" and "Revival in Canada" from *Healing from Heaven*, pp. 106-109, 115-119, by Lillian B. Yeomans, M.D., Gospel Publishing House, Springfield, Missouri, 1926.

"The Ministry of a Former Modernist Pastor" from *And Signs Followed*, pp. 56-62, by Charles S. Price, Logos International, Plainfield, N.J., revised edition 1972.

"The Revival Among the Girls of Mukti, India," quoted in *With Signs Following*, pp. 105-108, by Stanley H. Frodsham, Gospel Publishing House, Springfield, Missouri, 1946.